THE VITAL
CONGREGATION

EFFECTIVE
CHURCH
SERIES

HERB MILLER

THE VITAL
CONGREGATION

ABINGDON PRESS

Nashville

The Vital Congregation

Copyright © 1990 by Abingdon Press

All rights reserved.

This book is printed on acid-free paper.

Library of Congress Cataloging-in-Publication Data

MILLER, HERB.
  The vital congregation / Herb Miller.
    p. cm. — (Effective church series)
  Includes bibliographical references.
  ISBN 0-687-43796-2 (alk. paper)
  1. Pastoral theology. 2 Parishes. I. Title. II. Series.
BV4011.M495 1990
254—dc20   90-31095
                                        CIP

Scripture quotations, unless otherwise indicated, are from the Revised Standard Version of the Bible, copyright 1946, 1952, 1971 by the Division of Christian Education of the National Council of Churches of Christ in the U.S.A. Used by permission.

Acknowledgments

Ideas developed in a project with the Committee on Revitalization and New Church Development of the Memphis Conference of The United Methodist Church laid the foundation for this book. The committee's vision led to the production of a twelve-session video discussion program entitled *Developing a Vital Congregation* and its accompanying *Participant's Guide*.

Printed in the United States of America

Dedicated to Eva Metcalf
Whose lifetime of faithful devotion
to the service of God and congregations
has seldom been equaled.

CONTENTS

THE VITAL
CONGREGATION

FOREWORD

"Why?" is the most important question that church leaders can ask: "Why should we do this particular ministry task?" Failure to answer that question in a valid, biblical way wastes tons of leadership energy. Programmatic ships that should never have been built, sail out of the harbor for meaningless cruises.

After we ask why, inevitably we ask how: "How should we do this particular ministry task?" A young board chairman sat down in his pastor's office with a cup of coffee in hand. Upon the recommendation of a special task force, an important board decision the preceding evening had turned the church in a new direction. "I think our people want to be more effective in what the task force wants us to do," he said. "I just don't think they know how." Some form of that conversation happens in countless congregations every day. "Why?" is the most important question, but "how?" is the most frequently asked—and far more difficult—question to answer. Deftly deflecting a how question with "How do *you* think we should do it?" is a good counseling technique but not sufficient. Laypersons want and expect straight, helpful answers to their "how to do it" inquiries. If they do not get those answers, church work begun with high motivation and unselfishly donated time shipwrecks on the rocks of insufficient information.

Each volume of the Effective Church Series will help meet the need for "how to" answers in a specific area of church life. These books will provide clergy and laypersons with practical insights and methods that can increase their congregation's effectiveness in achieving God's purposes in every aspect of ministry: leadership, worship, Sunday school, membership care, biblical literacy, spiritual growth, small groups, evangelism, new member assimilation, prayer, youth work, singles work, young adult work, time management, stewardship, administration, community service, world mission, conflict resolution, writing skills.

This first volume stakes out the boundaries of the territory on which other books in the Effective Church Series will build. The vision of vital congregations and the need for more churches to live up to that term is washing across the beaches of all denominations. Yet, no one has told us exactly how to do that. By asking and answering diagnostic questions in ten areas of ministry, which are crucial to congregational vitality, this book does that. Readers and church groups can analyze and plan by looking at their congregation's image, which is reflected in the mirror of these questions.

Philosopher Alfred North Whitehead once advised a science student to seek simplicity and distrust it. Too few church leaders have heeded that counsel. The answer to "how" questions in megabyte, metropolitan churches is often quite different from the answer in a rural micro-sized church. Therefore, each volume in the Effective Church Series will take special care to illustrate the differences in how a method applies to congregations of different sizes and settings.

An insurance salesman stuck his head into a department store sales manager's office door and said, "You don't want to buy any insurance, do you?"

"Young man, who taught you how to sell? Don't ever ask that kind of question!" After a long lecture on salesmanship, in which he stressed that every customer's needs are different, the sales manager said, "Your problem is a lack of confidence. Give me an application blank. I'll buy some insurance from you to give you confidence in yourself." After completing the application, the sales manager gave the young salesman his closing lecture: "Now remember what I told you. Each customer is different. Figure out what each one really wants and needs. Then, you will know how to develop an approach that fits."

"That is exactly what I do," said the salesman. "What you have just observed is my approach for a sales manager. It works almost every time." This young man had organized his method to fit the situation.

The Effective Church Series will follow that pattern in providing practical methodology for churches of every size and setting. Eagerness to articulate universal principles will not override the necessity of applying them to different situations in seemingly contradictory ways.

The Effective Church Series is not theology or Bible study, but its "ideas that work" rest on biblical principles. Without that basis, method sharing feeds us a diet of cotton candy, sweet but devoid of nutrients. Three verses from Proverbs form the three-legged biblical stool on which this book and the entire Effective Church Series will sit. "Where there is no vision, the people perish" (29:18 KJV). "Without counsel plans go wrong" (15:22). "An intelligent mind acquires knowledge, and the ear of the wise seeks knowledge" (18:15).

Teachers of Victorian literature tell this story about Thomas Carlyle. He was dressed to go out for a Sunday speech before a large crowd. His mother was sitting beside the front door. As Carlyle passed her on his way out, she said to him, "And where might you be going, Thomas?"

"Mother," he replied, "I'm going to tell the people what is wrong with the world."

His mother responded with, "Aye, Thomas, but are you going to tell them what do about it?"

These volumes will tell what is right about the church as well as what is wrong, and what to do about both.

Herb Miller
Lubbock, Texas

13

INTRODUCTION

"I'm tired of hearing what's wrong with our denomination," said a loyal church member. "Let's emphasize the positive."

"I disagree," her friend responded. "Until we identify the negatives, how can we make them into positives?"

Which of these friends is right? Both, and neither! The key to health in any denomination is what happens in its congregations. Without effective congregations, regional and national ministries are like the chassis on a car from which someone has stolen all four wheels. Denominational offices provide support and direction, but congregations are where the rubber hits the road.

Why is "congregational vitality" a current buzz phrase in the mainline denominations whose membership has declined during the past twenty-five years? Partly because church leaders of these denominations attend the same national meetings. They catch ideas from one another. But also because the word "vitality" expresses a great truth. Without congregational vitality, the rubber that hits the road is a flat tire.

Congregations are as different from one another as snowflakes. Some are large; some are small. Some are in the open country; some live in the central city. Some have predominantly black members; some have predominantly white members; some have mostly Hispanic members or Asian members. In some, the members are mostly above age sixty-five; in others, the members are mostly below age forty-five. Is it possible to arrive at a definition and description of congregational vitality that fits them all? Yes, because congregations have one identical feature—their central goals. Different congregations use different methods and equipment—just as drivers use slightly different roads to arrive at their destination. But the goals toward which all congregations strive are identical. They come from the same road map—the Bible.

The ten basic characteristics in these ten chapters do not perfectly define and describe a vital congregation. Words are the final paint job on any body of truth, and different artists mix the paint differently. But this list is consistent with the biblical record and with research about today's congregations. It is, therefore, offered as a beginning framework. Revise and add to it from your own study and observations.

A vital congregation carries out the ministry of Jesus Christ by saying and doing what Jesus said and did. This ministry helps people (a) form a spiritual connection with God; (b) form a loving connection with other people; and (c) form a committed connection with great causes. In carrying out this ministry of Jesus Christ, the pastor-people ministry team in a vital congregation adopts principal attitudes and enacts methods which were operating in the early Christian communities. The vital congregation is a church that will:

1. develop lay and clergy leaders who model and communicate a vision of expectancy and hope regarding the future (Rom. 15:13).
2. spiritually nurture people in worship services (Acts 2:42).
3. help create a climate of Christian love and acceptance within the church (John 13:34-35).
4. involve large numbers of members in carrying out the ministry of Christ (I Cor. 12:4-9).

16

5. encourage people outside the church to experience a life-changing connection with Jesus Christ (Mark 1:17).
6. enthusiastically receive and assimilate new people into church life (Acts 2:47).
7. provide Sunday school and other small groups that offer Bible study and spiritual growth opportunities and meet many personal and social need (Eph. 4:12-14).
8. teach members how to develop a life of prayer (Luke 11:1).
9. encourage members to develop sacrificial stewardship of financial, time, and talent resources (I Cor. 12:4-7).
10. reach out to help heal the hurts and meet the needs of people in the church, community, and across the world (Matt. 24:45).

These ten characteristics of a vital congregation are not the only ones, but they are basic ones. Without these ten, a congregation cannot be fully effective in carrying out its ministry of saying and doing what Jesus said and did.

These chapters will help you put your congregation under a microscope and analyze its working parts. *Warning:* Avoid the temptation toward negativism inherent in all such processes. Every congregation is already vital in a number of ways. If it were not, it would not exist. People do not continue to participate in organizations that have no meaning. Find ways to celebrate the points at which your congregation is already experiencing vitality. Report these in your newsletter. Say them from the pulpit. Shout them from the rooftop. Continue balancing your attempts to repair weaknesses with a constant reiteration of present strengths. Otherwise, your congregation might accidentally stop doing the numerous things it is doing well.

On the other hand, do not gloss over points at which your church can strengthen its vitality. Few congregations are so perfect that some of the many factors presented in these pages do not speak a prophetic word to them. Examine the information. Discuss it with church leaders. Devise strategies. Let these pages do more than make a book; let them make a difference.

─I─
YOUR MOST IMPORTANT EMPLOYEE

Physician and author Bernie Siegel says that doctors can kill people with their words by telling them there is no hope. In one such instance, a physician told a woman with a brain tumor that she would be dead within a month and he could do nothing more for her. Twelve months after that, he happened to meet her on the street. They visited a few minutes, and she told him that she had traveled to another country for a treatment not yet approved for use in the United States. Her story ended on the happy note that she was now driving her car and playing the piano again. The physician responded with a lecture on the waste of time and money she was giving to that unproven treatment. The woman went home dejected. She died that night.[1]

Church leaders have a power equal to that in determining the future of their congregations. Vital congregations have at least ten characteristics. Each characteristic is important, but one of these ten can be imagined as the employee who unlocks the factory door. If he or she oversleeps, then the other nine cannot work. That key characteristic can be described in various ways, but the explanations boil down to one word—*hope. A vital congregation has lay and clergy leaders who model and communicate a vision of hope and expectancy regarding the future.*

Without hope, leaders will have insufficient motivation and energy to develop the other nine vital congregation characteristics. That is surely why the apostle Paul, when he wrote to the church in Rome at a difficult moment in history, urged them to abound in hope. "May the God of hope fill you with all joy and peace in believing, so that by the power of the Holy Spirit you may abound in hope" (Rom. 15:13). In correspondence with his problem church at Corinth, Paul lists hope as one of their three largest needs. Faith relates us to God in a positive way; love relates us to one another in a positive way; but hope relates us to our future in a positive way. Without hope, we stop being Christians and start becoming cynical skeptics about what God can do with our congregation's future. When that happens, creativity withers. Good intentions congeal into lethargy.

Rather than use the standard "Sincerely yours," a young pastor in North Carolina signs his letters, "Hope and confidence." He understands one of the deepest human needs. An old Arabian proverb says, "Those who have hope have everything." That is only a slight exaggeration. The attitude and atmosphere of hopefulness is a potent predeterminer of effectiveness in everything a congregation undertakes. The prime cause of failure in many church problems is the negative influence of leaders who sound as if they were baptized in dill-pickle juice.

What attitudes and methods must a congregation adopt in order to develop lay and clergy leaders who model and communicate a vision of expectancy and hope regarding the future? Numerous factors influence a congregation's supply of hope and expectancy. Holding these up as a printed mirror can significantly strengthen the amount of hope and expectancy in your congregation—and thus lock the door that lets the other nine employees come to work.

1. The positive attitude of the pastor. Nothing so immediately influences congregational direction, mood, and atmosphere as pastors who model a positive outlook on people, on reality, and on the future. A church cannot attract new people and energize its present members without a pastor who is excited about its potentialities. This is especially true for young adults. They look for excitement in all parts of their lives. If they find zero enthusiasm in their pastor, they look elsewhere for a place to invest their high ideals and energy levels.

Hopefulness is God's answer to Valium—and people who dispense this quality are addictive. What kinds of persons do you like to spend time with? Hopeful people or depressed, negative people? Which kind of pastor do people like to spend time with? Richard A. Zimmerman of Hershey Foods, one of America's outstanding chief executive officers, says, "Among the CEOs I know, the most successful ones have a very positive outlook. Every CEO has to be a cheerleader."[2] A positive pastor begins to mold a positive church in two or three years. A negative-thinking pastor remolds a positive church into a negative direction in two or three months.

2. The positive attitude of lay leadership. In slalom ski racing, the winners and those who come in second are separated by hundredths of a second. An Olympic Gold Medal winner says that there are no real secrets at the top of this highly competitive sport. Everyone is at about the same level of skiing skill. They all have the best equipment, know every inch of the course, and how they have to ski it to win. The critical factor that separates those who come in first from those who finish second is the racer's mental attitude. A nationwide, cross-industry business study revealed the same thing. The factor most significant in distinguishing top from moderate performers is attitude. Intelligence and skill are important, but attitude is the winning edge. That is equally and perhaps even more true in church leadership roles, where the motivation of workers is in no way related to paychecks.

The cara bird is a small parrot native to New Zealand. This pesky bird often eats the rubber out of windshield moldings on cars. If a window is down, a cara bird will also make lunch out of the upholstery. Many church problems show up like cara birds—unexpected and undeserved. A positive pastor is not enough. Without a positive attitude among lay leaders, the cara birds unravel a church's future.

Vital congregations do not try to exclude apathetic and negative persons from their membership. These people need to connect with God too. But a vital congregation limits the number of negative people who are placed in key lay leadership positions—or its vitality turns to vinegar. Positive things are more likely to happen with positive leaders.

Action Possibility: During a church board meeting ask the board members to list your congregation's greatest strengths. Collect these. Add up the ones that are identical. Publish the list. Urge lay leaders to overpower negativism by frequently citing these strengths in their conversations with one another and other members.

3. Positive conversational patterns among members.
A businesswoman who goes into the same restaurant every day for lunch usually orders the salad bar. When the waiter who usually works at her booth comes by, he often says, "Your salad looks so-o-o good!" One day, she realized what he was doing. He was strengthening her positive attitude about her choice of the salad bar for lunch, and her choice of this restaurant. She knew that a positive conversational pattern generates a positive mental attitude.

Moses and his refugee congregation followed a pillar of cloud by day and a pillar of fire by night (Exod. 13:21). Many modern congregations follow an opposite type of power. Their members habitually submerge themselves in a cloud of conversational pessimism. This leads them, not to the promised land, but to forty years of wilderness. When they gather for coffee at the doughnut shop, they habitually share bad news. "Did you hear what the preacher did to Jerry? Did you hear what a stupid thing they are putting in the new addition our church is building?" Jesus says we are defiled, not by what goes into our mouth but by what emerges (Matt. 15:11). That applies to churches too. What goes in the front door on Sunday morning damages them less than what comes out of members' mouths in idle moments.

These negative conversational habits are sometimes established by this year's church officers, but they can also originate from much earlier sources. In some churches, this dark cloud was created decades ago. Each new generation of church member picks up the pattern. Like the child in a family that is hypercritical of other people at the dinner table every evening, the church members have added that unfortunate trait to their conversational pattern without being aware of it.

How can leaders correct negative conversation habits in their church? When someone starts a hypercritical monologue, notice how quickly everyone in the group tends to follow suit. Like sheep flocking over a cliff, they jump at the chance to add a negative comment. When next that happens, test this method: After someone makes a negative statement, say, "But he really has some good qualities, too." Then illustrate one of these. If church leaders do this in every casual conversation where they get the opportunity, then many of the members will start emulating them instead of the negative people.

4. Conflict management ability among leaders. What is the quickest way to shrink a church? Conflict! Especially, long-term, under-the-table conflict. In some churches, slow growth is not the basic problem. Conflict is. Leaders are so busy trying to keep stressful personal relationships in balance that little energy remains for extroverted activity toward the unchurched. In some smaller towns, the public image of the congregation can become so damaged by rumors of feudin', fussin', and fightin', that more persons are repelled than attracted.

Conflict patterns in churches are like conflict patterns in marriages. Even though circumstances change and many years pass, they often keep reappearing. Church conflict patterns assume two general forms—conflict between pastor and members or conflict between members and members. Either of these patterns can keep repeating itself for decades. The characters change, but they are performing the same play. Most people are about as interested in participating in a quarreling church as they are in putting their hand in an electric blender. Vitality levels seldom rise to Olympic heights in such churches.

Action Possibility: In this instance and several others throughout many of the chapters, the Resources section in the back of the book contains a resource that has proved effective in countless congregations of many denominations. You may also want to call or write the appropriate departments in the national or regional offices of your denomination for a listing of the resources they produce in each of these areas of ministry.

5. Continue planning and goal setting. When asked for his secret, a hockey star replied, "I skate to where the puck is going to be, not to where it has been." Leaders in vital congregations understand and practice this principle. They engage in short-range and long-range planning, which helps them skate to where the puck is going, not to where it has been.

An older congregation has more past to consider. This is one of several reasons why new congregations tend to grow while older ones do not. Since they have no past, new churches focus on the future, set goals for it, and achieve results. Older congregations can focus on the future too—but only if their leaders move in that direction with great determination and intent.

In what direction do you think your congregation is focused—past or future? Ask yourself three questions: (1) Does our church have a mission statement that keeps us focused on our primary purpose? (2) During the past five years, have we consciously set short-range and long-range goals? (3) Have we in the past ten years used an outside consultant to help us see our strengths and build upon them with concrete goals and methods? In other words, what measures do we use to keep skating toward where the puck is going rather than toward where it has been?

Action Possibilities: See the Resources section in the back of the book for chapter 1.

6. The habit of "accentuating the positive" in all written communication. Rudyard Kipling said that words are the most powerful drug used by humankind. Much historical evidence supports that conviction. When someone asked Clement Attlee how Winston Churchill won the war, he replied, "He talked about it." Positive and negative syllables, more than anything else, rule the world. Communism did not capture two-fifths of the earth's land surface through tanks and missiles but through the writings of Karl Marx, a journalist. Mao did not take control of China through the actions of the Red Guard but through mass distribution of his "Little Red Book." The sixteenth-century Reformation moved through history on literary wheels. John Froben published Martin Luther's tracts in Wittenberg and circulated them all over Europe. Zwingli read them in Switzerland, Calvin in France, Cranmer in Britain, Ochino in Italy, Valdés in Spain—and the Reformation was under way.

Lutheran church historian Martin Marty noticed this sentence from Elie Wiesel hanging on a frame above a church leader's desk: "Words can sometimes, in moments of grace, attain the quality of deeds."[3] Leaders in vital congregations understand and practice the principle of positive communication. One seldom hears discouraging words in their newsletters, letters, and worship bulletins. They understand that newspapers profit from the publication of bad news, but churches move forward on good news.

A bumper sticker on the left back-bumper of a car in Lubbock, Texas, said: "Positively Lubbock." Another sticker on the right side of the same bumper said, "I'm mad, too, Eddie!" These opposite moods are seen in the written communication of many congregations but seldom in vital congregations.

7. The habit of remembering that "fun" is as important as work in producing good works. Late in the last century, a student pastor saw that a heavy snowfall required him to ice-skate down the river to get to his church. The elders were shocked. After the service, they asked for a private conference with him. They wanted to know why he would break the Sabbath by something as frivolous as ice-skating. They pondered his explanation with grave faces. Finally, they asked him if he had enjoyed skating down the river. He said that he had not, so they ruled that the apparent breach of conduct was permissible.[4]

Today's church watchers seldom witness such blatant anti-fun attitudes and behaviors. Yet churches score at greatly differing levels on the fun-factor scale. A traveling consultant says that he sometimes visits a church where no one has provided coffee, cookies, or other refreshments for the group meeting, which are part of the consultation proceedings. When refreshment is missing, he knows he is in a church where the fun factor is not understood. Additional observation will demonstrate that (a) attendance at group meetings is low in this church; (b) very little laughing and smiling takes place during worship services and other gatherings; and (c) the leaders tend to take themselves too seriously. All work and no play makes church people dull, and all work and no play makes church a dull place. When this happens, fewer and fewer persons show up, and those who come enjoy it less and less.

A low fun factor can stem from several different influences. The cause may be several years of behavioral modeling by one or more pastors who constantly exhibit an overserious countenance or a continually depressive mood state. Another source may be a stressful experience in the congregation's recent history—which causes the members to be on edge and fearful of facing conflict with one another. Another cause of low fun-factor levels may be an older median age of the members, many of whom were reared in an era when humor and joking in church were not considered proper behavior.

Action Possibility: Leaders can increase the fun factor in a church by (a) modeling more lighthearted behavior; (b) serving cookies and coffee at events, thereby providing people with more opportunities to socialize while they are doing church work; and (c) making fun times more intentionally a part of every church activity.

8. Significant levels of faith in God's power and providence. When certain blind men came to Jesus for healing, he asked them whether they believed that he was able to do it. After they said yes, he touched their eyes, saying, "According to your faith *and* trust *and* reliance [on the power invested in Me] be it done to you" (Matt. 9:28-29, Amplified Bible). Church leaders should select and use every effective method they can find, but nothing determines their congregation's future more than faith. Methods move muscles and systems and people and paper. Faith moves mountains.

What kept Paul going through all those shipwrecks and floggings? Not just optimism or Pollyanna self-suggestions about positive thinking. Not confidence in his own strength and ability. Paul was empowered by a hope born of believing in a power beyond himself. Hope is not optimism but an expectant attitude toward God. Paul did not say, "I can do all things." He said, "I can do all things in him who strengthens me" (Phil. 4:13).

If you believe in a God who loves you and empowers your future, then you receive hope. You know that your present painful circumstances are only temporary. No matter how knotty your problems, God can untie them. An exclamation point is at the end of whatever paragraph you are living out, not twenty dreary lines followed by a swamp of question marks.

A man went to buy a Rolls Royce. "It's the most famous car in the world," the salesman said. "Some Rolls Royces are still running after fifty years." As the man drove his purchase home, he realized that he had forgotten to find out how much horsepower the car had. When he went back to ask, the salesman couldn't find the answer anywhere in his materials, so he wired London, asking what the horsepower was. The telegram reply was one word—*adequate*. What Jesus told his first disciples still applies to us: "He who believes in me will also do the works that I do; and greater works than these will he do" (John 14:12). Leaders in vital congregations believe that when we undertake something for God that is within his will, we find the horsepower adequate.

————————— II —————————

THE GOD CONNECTION

Every human endeavor has a "main thing." Putting out fires is the main thing for fire fighters. They do other things, like fire prevention education, but a lack of effectiveness at their main thing spells institutional failure. Churches do many things, but their main thing is helping people connect with God. Worship is the primary way churches accomplish that main thing.

A few months before his death, in 1944, William Temple, broadcasting over the BBC, said that the world can be saved by only one thing—worship. He then defined worship: "To quicken the *conscience* by the holiness of God, to feed the *mind* with the truth of God. To purge the *imagination* with the beauty of God. To give the *heart* to the love of God. To devote the *will* to the purpose of God."[1] However you define it, worship is the main thing in helping people connect with God. Effective worship services are thus one of the crucial characteristics in building a more vital congregation. *The pastor-people ministry team in a vital congregation adopts attitudes and methods that spiritually nurture people in worship services.*

During the 1960s, Christian leaders became somewhat confused about the role of worship in Christian life. Jesus said that the main thing is to "love the Lord your God" (Matt. 22:37-38). He said the second thing is "to love your neighbor"

(Matt. 22:39). In the 1960s we tried to reverse these two imperatives. Some leaders objected that worship and expensive church buildings for worship were self-serving, that the main thing was to love people. The effort got some good things done, but it eroded the church's ability to do its main thing. We get the power to love people from our love of God. The reverse does not work. When we invert the order of these two elements of the Great Commandment, we eventually lose the power to do either.

Evidence for the central role of worship in a vital congregation appears in both the biblical record and modern research. The book of Acts tells us that the first disciples "devoted themselves to the apostles' teaching and fellowship, to the breaking of bread and the prayers" (Acts 2:42). The apostle Paul warns new Christians against "neglecting to meet together, as is the habit of some" (Heb. 10:25).

A positive, uplifting worship service ranks among the top six reasons why people say they join growing congregations (on a list of forty-eight).[2] Another study reports that 82.7 percent of new members in all congregations rate the quality of the worship service as an important reason for joining.[3] In still another study, 64 percent of the church dropouts declared that the "worship service is not meaningful" was a major cause.[4]

What, then, are the qualities that one usually finds in the worship service of a vital congregation? If we viewed videotapes of worship in two dozen rapidly growing churches of every size, would we see similar factors? Yes, we would. Asking and answering the following questions can help us to hold a constructive mirror up to our own worship service.

1. Does our worship service communicate warmth, friendliness, and a family-type atmosphere?

Pastors of several hundred significantly growing congregations across North America were asked what qualities they strive for in their worship service. The following phrases typify their responses: Warmth as well as dignity; a relaxed dignity; a friendly type of worship without its being too folksy or losing dignity; warm formality; joy with dignity, expressed affection, a happy, upbeat climate; warmth and flexibility; a friendly family life atmosphere. These important qualities become more clear when we remember that approximately 70 percent of first-time worship visitors in every congregation are tense. They fear doing the wrong thing and sitting in the wrong place. They want to avoid looking odd. An atmosphere of warmth and friendliness reduces their anxiety.

While describing the service in her declining church, a laywoman said, "Our congregation's formal formality has become cold formality. If people wanted that, they would do their worshiping in a doctor's waiting room." People look for the worship services that communicate a warm, family feeling. Is this because people who experienced warmth in their childhood want to re-experience it in their church family? Is it because people who did not experience warmth and acceptance in their formative years have been searching for it all their lives? Whatever the reason, when they meet it in a church sanctuary, they come back for more.

Action Possibilities: See the Resources section for chapter 2.

2. Does the leader of our worship service communicate warmth, friendliness, and enthusiasm?

The attitude of the worship leader is immediately copied by the worshipers. The only thing more contagious than enthusiasm is apathy. The only thing more contagious than apathy is negativism. If you are the worship leader, the feelings you have in your mind, facial features, and voice tone are highly contagious. Whatever you have, everyone in the room is going to catch. T. Garrott Benjamin, Jr., pastor of a fast-growing black congregation in Indianapolis, says:

When you bring them, they have got to come to something. The pastor has a tremendous responsibility in setting the tone for a church. Man is both cerebral and somatic. He both thinks with his mind and feels with his heart and soul. So, enthusiasm is a key. People come here with all kinds of problems. Man, they want some enthusiasm. They want somebody to pick them up. And sometimes from our pulpits we have a tendency to depress people. If we can get excited about the Prince of Wales, can't we get excited about the Prince of Peace?[5]

Many components contribute to the total mix of a worship service experience: friendliness and enthusiasm of the congregation, quality of the music, form and flow of the service, the building's architecture, the decor of the sanctuary, the bulletin's appearance, evidence of active programming, availability of parking, and the church reputation in the community. Nothing, however, influences the worship service as much as the personality and style of the pastor. He or she does not communicate that as much by the content of what is said as by how it is said.

3. Does our worship service project an atmosphere of caring and concern for the needs of people?

The sharing of joys and concerns in morning worship is one of the ways many pastors of growing churches achieve a family feeling. One pastor says, "Many people are attracted by the informal sharing of joys and concerns prior to the prelude." Another pastor says, "Providing a time for sharing joys and needs before the morning prayer is important to us. We are careful not to hurry that time, but let all share. And they do." Still another says, "I begin with a brief 'greetings and announcements' on the lower level before we begin our worship *per se*. We sometimes sing 'Happy Birthday' to someone. Such intimacy, I believe, allows the Spirit to be more effective in its work in our worship experience."[6]

4. Does our worship service have variety and innovation within a general format that remains similar each week?

Boredom is the root of much evil in church life. Nowhere is this more true than in worship. Something new grabs attention and recharges commitment. Sameness, sameness, sameness sends the mind to the sandman! Growing churches

31

conquer boredom in worship by creatively varying the parts of a general format that remains the same each week. Pastors describe this process with phrases like this: structured worship with variations within that structure; a variety of individual worship expressions; innovative alterations in the order of worship each quarter to keep it from becoming stale; very traditional, but with regular innovations.

Vital congregations build structured variety into worship. Dying churches carve out routines and ruts. The greater the average age of members, the harder leaders must struggle to achieve variety. More than 65 percent of persons in many mainline denominations are over the age of fifty. The natural pressure of majority opinion therefore runs many worship services downhill toward a resistance to change. This soon becomes a self-fulfilling preference. After a few years, the worship services may be unable to attract younger members.

5. Is our worship indigenous to the culture of our community?

The dictionary defines *indigenous* as "having originated in and being produced, growing, living, or occurring naturally in a particular region or environment." Everyone recognizes the necessity of indigenous worship on the world's mission fields. Less well recognized is how that same principle applies to the various subcultures across North America. People in a small town in upstate New York may appreciate a slightly different type of worship service than people who retire in Arizona. Worship leaders unaware of or uncaring about worship preferences indigenous to their particular culture collect more empty pews than people. Instead of trying to impose ideas gleaned from seminary days or former pastorates, leaders of vital congregations do what works in this time and place. Their ancestors did the same thing on the American frontier. Indigenous worship was one of the principal reasons for the rapid growth of the nineteenth-century mainline denominations. They cut the worship cloth to fit the people, not the people to fit the pastor's European preferences.

6. Does the atmosphere of our worship service include humor?

A parishioner handed his pastor a Christmas gift—two books by "Peanuts" cartoonist Charles Schulz. "Sorry I didn't get them wrapped," the man apologized. "That's o.k.," the pastor replied, noting that the humorous books had been purchased in a drugstore and were in a prescription sack. "This is a prescription all of us need—a little more humor in our lives."

Nowhere is that observation more accurate than in worship services. The pastor of one growing congregation says that humor is a big factor in communicating acceptance. Another pastor believes that humor is a symbolic indication that, here, you do not have to worry about how you look or what you say—which is another way of saying that you belong. Still another pastor says, "An effective worship service focuses on humor, hope, and enthusiasm." Worship leaders should act like elevator operators who are helping to raise spirits to God's floor of optimism and joy. So, smile. Many people who attend worship services are stressed and depressed. They need an antidote, not more poison.

A sense of humor or the lack of one also says something about the worship leader's intelligence quotient. Years ago, studies at Purdue University and Vassar College proved conclusively that an appreciation of humor corresponds with keen intelligence. People less well-endowed intellectually generally find fewer things that they consider amusing. Worship leaders should, of course, avoid the extremes of tiresome punsterism and stand-up comedy. But try not to take yourself so seriously that it registers on your face. As well as depressing and boring the congregation, such a demeanor may subtly tell them that you are not too bright!

7. Does our worship service include something for children?

Today's young adults appreciate institutions that emphasize family qualities and values. They grew up in a culture focused on increasing respect for each *individual person* and a desire to meet his and her needs. The parents and grandparents of these young adults grew up in a culture that focused on meeting the needs of the *majority* of persons in a particular group. These two trends—family values and meeting individual needs—have increased the number of congregations that use a children's sermon or children's church, or both. These churches are not just following a fad; they are responding to a deeply felt need. Families are disintegrating at the fastest rate in recorded history. By vividly saying through the components of a worship service, "We care about every member of the family," you offer good news.

8. Is the tempo of the music in our worship service upbeat and fast moving?

Music is 40 percent of the service. The tempo therefore has the power to either resurrect or murder all the other parts. When the music is upbeat, visitors get a feeling of liveliness and creativity. When the music drags, visitors get the impression of stale, solemn sameness. Alive music arouses enthusiasm (the word *enthusiasm* means "filled with God"). Dead music arouses sleepiness. People who grew up on seven hours of T.V. each day are accustomed to watching a week go by in thirty minutes and a year in one hour. A hymn that drags can seem like a tiresome eternity and destroy any hope of joy in the noise that we make to the Lord.

Smaller congregations often find it difficult to communicate constructively in ways that increase the speed of snail pace organists. Such persons are often deeply dedicated donors with many years of service. Some instrumentalists become increasingly resistant to new pastors who think that the worship service should meet the spiritual needs of the worshipers rather than those of the musicians.

Action Possibility: Many organists are not as resistant to insights as they are insulated from them. As their years of serving multiply, even their close friends find it difficult to work a phrase into a conversation, such as, "You are playing too slowly." Ask the organist to select four persons of four different ages from the congregation (not from the choir). The organist asks these four persons to meet with him or her for five minutes following worship once a month. Each month, the organist keeps asking this group, "How is the tempo going?" Feedback is the breakfast of champions. But if you never ask, you never get fed. This system closes the feedback loop in a positive way. Because the organist is in control of the evaluation, he or she is likely to receive the data with appreciation rather than resentment.

9. Do the majority of our members know the hymns we sing in worship?

One-third to three-fourths of the people who have joined every congregation in the United States since 1980 came from some other denominational family. Because of this new "denominational switching ecumenism," church leaders cannot expect all the worshipers to know the same hymns as they did three decades ago. The bottom-line question about church music is, Does it move people closer to God? Worshipers who are shut out of personal participation because they do not know a hymn can hardly answer that question in the affirmative.

Action Possibility: To overcome the problem of accidentally singing hymns that the congregation does not know, appoint a task force of eight persons, evenly distributed across the age range of twenty through eighty. Ask this group to meet once or twice and go through the hymnbook. With each hymn, ask, Do you know this hymn? If six out of the eight know the hymn, the congregation probably does. If fewer than six know the hymn, the worshipers will have a tough time singing it. Out of this procedure, compile a list entitled "All the Hymns We Presently Know." Take this list to whoever selects the hymns for each Sunday. In some churches, the pastor chooses. In other churches choices are determined by the choir director, the organist, or the worship committee chairperson. Whoever it is, threaten him or her with potential loss of life or limb if the list is not used. This procedure does not prevent leaders from teaching new hymns *intentionally*, perhaps with an occasional "hymn of the month." But it protects them from trying to teach unfamiliar hymns *accidentally* and always failing. So what if the "approved hymn list" contains only seventy hymns? No one is going to come up after church and say, "We just sang that hymn nine weeks ago." Their memories are not that good. Besides, they are in worship to get in touch with the Transcendent, not to increase their musical repertoire.

10. Does our worship music meet the needs of more than one generation and more than one kind of person?

Almost every congregation contains three musical generations each Sunday morning. One group (many of whom are over the age of forty) prefers "classic" hymns, like "The Church's One Foundation." A second group (many of whom are over sixty years of age) likes music from the gospel era, much of which was written between 1900 and 1935. This music was popular when these people were young, the period when people develop their likes and dislikes for music. A third group (many of whom are under age forty) enjoys today's Christian hymns, many of which were written or set to a different tune after 1960. They also like choral responses. This age group grew up with faster, rhythmic tunes and the tones of guitars, saxophones, and drums. Growing churches try to meet the musical needs of all three groups of people *in every service*, not just occasionally. They know that focusing on one kind of hymn results in several persons leaving the service who feel as if they have not been to church. Worship and music leaders who insist on serving only one kind of worshiper will, after ten or twenty years, end up with only that kind of person in their services.

Action Possibility: Experiment for a few months with a hymn selection formula that involves one classic hymn to open the service, one hymn selected from the gospel era, and one from today's church music scene. Sprinkle in some additional choral responses of a modern variety. Evaluate with a questionnaire circulated among morning worship attenders.

11. *Is our worship service spiritually focused?*

Roland Walker for many years chaired the religion department at Ohio Wesleyan University. One morning at 2:30, a student prankster phoned him, asked "Is God there?" and hung up. When Walker told about the incident in a sermon at Grey Chapel, he said it was an excellent question and then asked the academic community how they would answer it.[7]

Congregations can reflect beneficially on that question with regard to their worship services. Is God there? Are the worship services spiritually focused? People who attend church are looking for contact with God. If they were only looking for a pleasant experience with other people, then they would attend a football game. If they were looking only for a chance to help a good cause, then they would give to the Cancer Fund.

Many experts feel that the remarkable growth of Christianity in Africa and South America is related to how the congregations there use their time. They focus primarily on worship, Bible study, and prayer. By contrast, congregations in the declining mainline denominations in the United States seem more focused on fellowship events, community service, and committee work. Those differences seem subtle to the casual observer, but their results are dramatically different. The same is true in the forms of the worship service. Vital congregations focus on the vertical relationship with God. A positive horizontal relationship with people is not unimportant to vital congregations. But their leaders know that strengthening the vertical lifts the horizontal relations among members to higher levels of caregiving and love, while the reverse is not necessarily true.

12. *Is our worship service and preaching biblically centered?*

Bernard Manning defined preaching as "the manifestation of the Incarnate Word, from the Written Word, by the Spoken Word."[8] Preaching that loses connection with its foundation in biblical authority loses voltage and becomes

37

speaking instead of preaching. The congregation notices the difference more quickly than does the preacher. They do not know how to define what has happened, but they know how to depart from it and not return.

Many persons in our secular society believe far more in the authority of the Bible than they did ten years ago. Ironically, many young adults seem to believe in this authority more than many pastors. They respond far more positively to "biblical" preaching than the generation immediately preceding them. These young adults define a biblical sermon as one that contains a high percentage of biblical content. They expect the central point of the sermon to grow out of the biblical text itself, instead of developing as a philosophical point with a biblical text thrown in as an illustration. The first *Discipline* published by the Methodists in America said, "A peculiar blessing accompanies the public reading as well as preaching the word of God to attentive, believing souls. And in these days of infidelity, nothing should be omitted, which may lead the people to the love of the holy bible."[9] Today's young adults have rediscovered that lost love. Vital congregations know that and design their worship services accordingly.

13. If we have more than one morning worship service, are they different from each other?

Multiple worship services enable a congregation to better meet the needs of different types of people. Adding a second worship service usually increases total attendance by 5 to 15 percent. If the second service is not a copy-machine duplicate of the first one, then the increased attendance is usually higher. A simple principle stands behind that universal statistic: Offer more options, and you get larger responses. People who are intimidated by large crowds can join the church during the early service. Those who like informal worship can attend another service. People who like something shorter can meet their need. Most young adults were reared in large school-systems. They experience multiple options while shopping. They expect to have the same choices available in church life. Church leaders who decide that these options are not important are deciding against growth and vitality.

14. Is the length of worship service appropriate?

Most mainline churches that grow numerically hold their worship service length to sixty minutes. Their worship leaders understand how the average worship visitor thinks—especially if he is, for example, a husband who is present because of the urging of his wife, rather than his own inclination. This person is far more concerned than the regular member about the time length of church services. As the clock pushes past an hour, he fidgets. At ten minutes past, he grows slightly irritated. When it hits one hour and fifteen minutes, he begins feeling cheated. If the service runs thirty minutes past the hour, then he will likely leave the building with more disgruntlement than peace in his soul. Someone has committed grand larceny against his personal time off! Next week, the visiting family may try a church where the pastor is more sensitive about the stewardship of time.

Exceptions to this sixty-minute principle are seen in congregations of some denominations or ethnic settings. Black or Hispanic churches, for example, often find a longer service effective. Leaders must therefore ask themselves, Does our service length fit the people and the community in which we minister?

Generally speaking, however, if the worship of God is not achieved in one hour, the team seldom scores a touchdown during the overtime period. Tighten up. Eliminate wasted time (which usually happens during the offering, communion, announcements, sermonic redundancy, and by habitually starting the service five to seven minutes late). Ask yourself whether the pastor and worship leader are actively *in charge* of when the service begins? Or, are they at the mercy of a worship leader or someone in the choir who is habitually late?

15. Does our church use children and youth in lighting candles or in other worship functions?

Personal involvement significantly increases the sense of meaning that children and youth obtain from the worship experience. Although some churches are too large to provide for these opportunities, many churches need only to become more intentional in this matter. A few minutes of discussion by the appropriate committee often surfaces some excellent new possibilities.

16. Does our church have a well-trained group of greeters who serve after as well as prior to the worship service?

The two most commonly used methods for greeter recruitment are usually failures. One method assigns this task to all church members by alphabetical rotation of last names. The other method gives it to a particular group of church officers. With either system, one-half of the group does not wish to do this work and therefore does it halfheartedly. "I didn't sign on for this," they say. One-half of the remaining one-half of the group in either system lacks the personality skills for this work. Therefore, only one-fourth of the people in either system do the greeting effectively.

Action Possibilities:

• Develop a greeter corps of persons who have volunteered or have been selected for this ministry. Purchase plastic name tags for this greeter corps. Ask that two members of the corps serve at each door before as well as after worship.

• In large buildings, post maps at each door so that greeters can use these maps in directing first-time visitors to the nursery or to restrooms.

17. Do our worship visitors receive a friendly welcome by persons other than the official greeters?

What happens when worship visitors are welcomed at the door but feel no spirit of friendliness in the pews? They evaluate the congregation negatively.

Action Possibilities:

• Ask church officers and perhaps other active members to assume responsibility for a particular pew or pews in the area of the sanctuary where they usually sit during worship each Sunday. Ask them to agree to welcome and get acquainted with any strangers who appear in these pews. This approach will guarantee that no one can leave our worship service and complain to their friends, "Not a single person spoke to me."

• The after-worship coffee fellowship is another opportunity for improving a congregation's warmth and friendliness quotient. Ask members and persons from the greeter corps to invite visitors to stay for coffee after worship. When that happens, visitors are likely to get acquainted with several members and feel much more like returning.

• Still another fellowship-enhancing technique is the plastic name tags that are becoming popular, especially in larger congregations. These plastic introducers help new members and older members alike to learn names more quickly, and thus, tend to increase fellowship.

18. Are our nursery space and furniture adequate to satisfy the average young-adult parent?

Most of the people who bring infants and toddlers to our church grew up in far better housing than their parents and grandparents. These young adults are accustomed to carpeting in their homes and much better furnishings than the generations just before them. Because of this, and because many young adults "shop" for a church after they move to town, what visitors with infants find in the nursery can be just as important as what they find in the worship service. The nursery can thus determine whether they return, join, and keep attending.

Action Possibility: If the church nursery space and furniture are not adequate, appoint a committee of three to six young mothers to make recommendations to the property committee for putting the furniture and room into A-1 condition. Remind the church board that money invested in the nursery always comes back into the church treasury. This investment produces increases in giving from new young couples who attend and join because you have a good nursery.

19. Is our nursery staffing system adequate to satisfy the average young-adult parent?

Only under very rare circumstances does a volunteer, unpaid nursery staff prove effective. Free staff members usually cost the church more money than they save it. The financial giving lost when only one young family per year decides not to return for a second visit, and thereby fails to begin attending regularly, easily pays for a nursery attendant.

Hire someone who is not a member of your congregation. If the person does not prove satisfactory, dismissal can occur without a rift in the church family.

Hire an older person. Young adults have more confidence in grandmotherly types than in high schoolers.

20. Does our church's off-street parking, along with the street parking adjacent to our property, total one-half of the average worship attendance in our largest morning worship service?

Insufficient parking spaces strangle worship attendance. How do we know this is true? Because many churches suffering this invisible strangulation have purchased lots to add parking spots and noted that their worship attendance instantly increased.

Action Possibilities:

• Adding an earlier worship service can reduce the parking pressure.

• Ask key leaders to make the sacrifice of parking at a greater distance so that older persons can park closer.

• Leaders often defend their lack of parking spaces by saying, "We cannot afford to buy more lots for parking. It is too expensive." This is inevitably the wrong conclusion. Divide your total offerings for a year by our average morning worship attendance. The resulting figure is usually somewhere between $500 and $1,400 annually (the larger the church, the higher the average giving per worship attender per year). For the purpose of illustration, let us say that this figure for your church is $800. If your worship attendance is being invisibly reduced because of inadequate parking, this loss is costing your church an average of $1,600 per year for every parking space which would have been used had it been there (on the average, people attend worship two per car). In ten years, that cost totals $16,000 per parking space. So the question board members should ask is never, Can we afford more parking spaces? The more appropriate question is always, How much is our church losing in contributions each year because of our failure to provide adequate parking?

21. Is the seating space adequate for our worship service?

In most cases, your seating is adequate if less than 85 percent capacity of the seats are filled on the average Sunday. If your sanctuary is usually more full than 85 percent, you have three options: (1) add an additional worship service to create more space; (2) build a larger worship area to create more space; or (3) be satisfied with fewer people in worship and lower offerings than if you had adequate space.

A church near a busy interstate highway in the Western United States built a new building. The roof line of the beautiful sanctuary pointed upward toward the front, the side nearest the highway. Before completion, they ran out of money. The tall spire—the architect's marvelous way of pointing the viewer toward God—was left off. Thus, for thousands of passersby, the building points upward every day to an absent spire.

Architecture is not, however, the primary way churches point people to God. Worship is. A church that fails to point people to God with its worship service is like a spireless building. Without the spiritual dimension provided in worship, churches lack the one essential ingredient that distinguishes them from the other important institutions in town.

III

CLIMATE CONTROLS THE CROPS

A pastor who grew up in Miami moved to Iowa. As he was getting acquainted with a young farmer in the congregation, he said, "Tell me why there is so much corn in Iowa and so little in some other parts of the country."

"It's mainly the difference in climate and soil conditions," the farmer replied. "You see the same thing in your work. Some churches are healthy and active, with a lot of new members joining. In other congregations, you see the opposite. Because the climate and soil conditions are different, the crops are different."

Church research verifies that farmer's observation. The church climate controls the crops and one of the climate characteristics most essential to growing a vital congregation is love and acceptance. Visitors in these churches report a quality of "feeling at home," which they say was absent from many other congregations they visited. The psychological environment is supportive, noncritical, and reassuring. *The pastor-people ministry team in a vital congregation adopts attitudes and enacts methods which help create a climate of Christian love and acceptance.*

Contrary to popular folk wisdom, this climate is not related to church size. Some small churches have it; other small churches feel cold and aloof. Some giant-sized churches have it; other large churches are impersonal and staid. Victor Hugo said that the supreme happiness of life is the conviction that we are loved. Churches of every size, when operating at optimum climate conditions, tell us that God loves us. They give us the opportunity to experience love from others. Jesus puts the element of love and acceptance this way: "A new commandment I give to you, that you love one another; even as I have loved you, that you also love one another. By this all men will know that you are my disciples, if you have love for one another" (John 13:34-35). Fourteen times in the New Testament we are told to "love one another."

Through a variety of verbs, the New Testament writers expanded on what they meant by this phrase, "Love one another": to be kind to, forgive, listen to, pray for, serve, care for, confess to, bear burdens of, be members of, strengthen, and have fellowship. That is surely why Paul says that among the three Christian behaviors (faith, hope, and love), love is the greatest (I Cor. 13:13). Faith and hope are invisible inner qualities; love is external and observable. Faith and hope feel and think; love has hands that reach out to help and give.

The degree to which a congregation possesses a climate of love and acceptance so essential for vitality and growth is determined by the degree to which ten factors are present. By asking and answering the following questions, church leaders can analyze the strength of these factors in their congregations.

1. Do most of our members go out of their way to greet and talk with visitors in the worship service?

Great preaching without warmth and friendliness among the worshipers is like eating lobster from a tin pie-pan. In some congregations, a stranger cannot get far into the building without a friendly greeting from several people. Other congregations give you the feeling of attending church in an elevator. No one speaks, nor do they seem to feel that they should. They act as if everyone here is headed for a different floor on business that does not require social interaction. Unfortunately, churches offering a cold shoulder are like individual persons with a cold shoulder. They are often the last to learn how they come across to those around them.

Action Possibilities:

• Conduct individual interviews (either by phone or in person) with all the adults who have joined your church during the last two years. Tell these new members that you are gathering information that will help in making plans to improve your church. Ask them to pick the answer that is closest to accurate among the multiple-choice options in these two questions:

1. The first two times you visited our worship service, which of the following best described the atmosphere: (a) extremely warm and friendly; (b) friendly; (c) pleasant but somewhat distant; or (d) cold and aloof?
2. The first few times you visited our church's worship service, fellowship dinners, or other meetings, which of the following best describes what happened: (a) You found yourself standing or sitting alone while other members talked with one another; (b) A few persons spoke in a courteous way, but left you to break into circles of conversation on your own initiative; (c) One or two persons went out of their way to include you, but the others acted as if you were not there; or (d) Everyone included you in their group and conversational circles as if you had been a member forever.

Do not ask people these questions in a group setting, since under those circumstances many people tend to give a nice answer rather than an accurate answer. Do not ask these questions of people who have been members longer than two years. Most people who have been members that long feel so much a part of the church family that they have completely forgotten how they felt on their first visits.

• The pastor of a small-membership congregation in Alabama says that they have a system whereby all first-time visitors are invited to lunch by one of the members. He says visitors usually cannot accept that invitation because they have other plans. But that gives the inviter the opportunity to say, "What about next Sunday?" The visiting individual or family, who quite naturally respond with a "Yes," are thereby committing themselves to return to worship the following week, and are possibly starting a habit. The church has seen significant membership growth as a result of this love and acceptance.

2. Do the people who answer the telephone in our church office communicate warmth, friendliness, and caring concern?

After sweeping the country in the 1970s, the bright yellow smiley face has now taken residence at European and American stores like Bloomingdale's. They cannot get enough of T-shirts and tote bags featuring the two dots for eyes and a wide smile. This ubiquitous symbol of niceness and good spirit will undoubtedly keep returning to the marketplace again and again. It sends a signal. It props up our downness with upness. It improves the atmosphere inside our heads, hearts, and lives.

The way that persons in an office answer the telephone has the same amazing capacity for instantly improving or impairing our attitude. No amount of warmth from the pastor or the members compensates for a cold, indifferent personality on the church phone. One church secretary said, "I put a smiley face sticker on my phone to remind me to put a smiley face on my voice when I pick the receiver up."

Action Possibilities:

● The telephone company may have helpful printed material, which you can pass along to church staff members. A business person in your group may have useful material.

● The following tips are among the most important in improving telephone manners. Type them on cards and tape them on the church phones. (a) Always smile when you answer the phone. It improves your animation and warmth. (b) Raise your voice slightly when answering the phone. You sound as if you are in a better mood. (c) Do not do anything with the paperwork on your desk while you are talking on the phone. It makes you come across as preoccupied with your own problems. (d) When you pick up the phone, imagine that someone may be calling to tell you that you have won a five-million-dollar sweepstakes. This significantly improves your sense of anticipation.

3. Do the laypersons who are in key offices and leadership roles in our congregation usually seem willing to listen to people who share problems and new ideas?

A visitor in a small church found folded in her worship bulletin a sheet titled "Garbage Removal Responsibility List." She scanned the names listed under each of the twelve months of the coming year. Then she saw what it was for. A note at the bottom of the page explained the sheet: "Take plastic bags from cans in the kitchen—tie ends—place in front of church—anytime Sunday after church." Everyone who actively participates in any aspect of church life automatically gets on the garbage removal responsibility list. In the same way, human relationships, especially in groups, exhibit an endless untidiness. People who are unwilling to hear about problems, listen to complaints, and sort through old ideas to see if they can be recycled will find themselves feeling uneasy much of the time.

Experts at this task remind us that most people do not need a complete solution to all their complaints. They need to feel that someone is willing to listen to them and trying to understand how they feel. Church members who exhibit warmth, care, sensitivity, affirmation, and empathy are like a magnet. They tend to attract more and more people with whom to practice these skills. At the other extreme, parishioners are repelled by churches whose leaders will not listen to problems and new ideas. Have you ever met anyone who did not think his or her complaint was valid? Have you known anyone who did not think his or her new ideas had some significance? Leaders in vital congregations recognize that this desire for acceptance is deeply rooted in human nature, and they exhibit the attitude of receptivity required to meet this need.

4. Do our members and those who are in leadership roles usually communicate God's love, grace, and acceptance to people who do not meet their moral, ethical, or religious standards?

In some congregations, purity of doctrine has become more important than purity of love. The Good News, which the Bible directs us to share, has become Good Rules we are trying to enforce. This old tension derives from two seemingly opposite tenets of Christianity—God's judgment and God's grace. The apostle Paul met this tension in the Jerusalem council meeting, which is described in Acts 15. The Jewish Christians wanted to enforce the Jewish ritual of circumcision on all new Christians. Paul answered their demand with the same love and acceptance that he employed to handle the conflict in the Corinthian Church, which is described in II Corinthians 13.

Love is still the first rule of effective Christianity and vital churches—not the second rule. If we practice our primary rule of love, people will consider accepting our high standards of doctrine, morals, and ethics. If we do not practice that first rule, we erect barricades that block many people from entering the highway that leads to changed lives. John Wesley tended to ignore the small differences in personal doctrinal opinions. He said that all he asked was whether a person believed in Jesus Christ. If that person did, he said that was enough. Leaders in many congregations need to relearn Wesley's habit.

5. Does our church have a strong sense of esprit de corps?

The French term *esprit de corps* means that we have frequent opportunities to have fun while working to achieve common goals. The sense of closeness described by members of vital congregations derives from more than commonly held religious beliefs and from attending worship together; it comes from working together to do what they feel God has called them to do in his kingdom of love. Many of the Christians who worship together but never work together will eventually come unglued from the church and cease to worship together.

6. Do our church leaders have the habit of praising instead of blaming people?

Jonathan Swift said that we have just enough religion to make us hate, but not enough to make us love one another.[1] Although this generalization does not apply to all Christians, it describes some of us. The "blaming syndrome" is among the most destructive of maladies observed in churches. We have all seen how this malady operates in some family units. Parental speech patterns are filled with phrases such as: "It's his fault. It's her fault. It's their fault. It's your fault." Some church families, and some church leaders, have a similar blaming syndrome as their characteristic way of thinking and behaving. Unfortunately, the blamer is usually the last person to realize this fault and the last person to realize that a thimbleful of affirmation usually does more good than a truckload of blame.

The habit of blaming rather than praising people tends to produce several destructive results: (a) frequent conflict over small issues; (b) difficulty in getting people to assume offices and responsibilities in the church, because they know they will be strongly criticized for how they do their jobs; (c) reduction of creativity and innovation, as the fear of criticism causes both pastor and people to "play it safe" and do the same things the same way; and (d) a series of short pastorates, as each minister becomes the target of and then the victim of members who keep trying to make the church perfect by blaming the pastor for everything that goes wrong.

7. Do our adult classes have designated greeters who are responsible for helping visitors feel at home?

There is only one thing worse than visiting a church where no one speaks to you—visiting a Sunday school class where no one speaks to you and helps you feel at home.

Action Possibility: Effective greeters are as important in adult Sunday school classes as they are in worship services.

Select one or more individuals in each class to serve as official greeters. These should be persons who meet people easily and are good at conversational small talk. Ask these greeters to be there fifteen minutes early each Sunday. Visitors are sometimes the only people who arrive early for Sunday school— only to be greeted by a dark, empty room.

8. Does our church have an organized system by which our members, who are shut-ins or have long-term illnesses, are visited regularly and remembered in special ways?

A coffee-drinking regular at a nearby restaurant, Carrows, was surprised at the appearance of a long row of little brown bears for sale. Each of the fuzzy animals had a sign on the front: "Carrows Cares!" The sign above them said "Adopt me. $4.95." The customer was even more amazed at how fast the "Care Bears" sold. Surely, he thought, this is solid proof of how much people in our society value and want relationships. Triple that need for people in long-term illness and nursing homes. When a frail person has lost a major personal identity and esteem factor—meaningful work—relationships are all that is left.

Care for the frail is one of those many areas in church life where something that is everyone's responsibility becomes no one's responsibility. Nor is delegating this task to the pastor a sufficient plan. Yes, people need care and concern from the pastor, but they also need it from other people in the church. If we do not have some simple plan for doing that, it will not consistently happen. And vitality is sapped from the congregation.

9. Does our church have an organized program which ensures that our members feel loved and supported by other lay persons during times of stress, such as hospitalization and bereavement?

Researchers at the University of Missouri at Columbia discovered that the people in their study who lived longest were those who helped others and enjoyed social relationships.[2] And yet, times of stress is another of those areas where many churches substitute discussing the need for meeting the need. The widespread adoption of geographical shepherding programs during the last twenty years—and the subsequent failure and abandonment of 90 percent of those geographical plans—has made most church leaders feel that nothing can be done about this matter. This is an inaccurate assumption.

A mother and daughter were having lunch after some shopping. Sitting near them was an older woman who ate silently and appeared to be extremely unhappy.

As they got up to leave, the mother walked over to the woman and said, "Excuse me, but you remind me so much of my mother. Would you mind if I gave you a hug?"

The older woman beamed and gratefully accepted the hug. It obviously made her feel much better.

"That was really sweet, Mom," the daughter said when they got outside, "but I didn't think she looked at all like Grandma."

"Nor did I," said the mother cheerfully.

Some people just seem to have a knack for cheering others up. Vital congregations set up organized systems by which members with this kind of love can use it to hug the many people who need one.

Action Possibilities:

• Organize a Care Corps of ten to twenty persons who meet monthly with the pastor or pastors and accept assignments for calling on people who are shutins, hospitalized, in grief, or suffering other stress. Avoid setting this up on a geographical basis, because those systems rarely work. If you divide the church into "flocks," allow Care Corps members to select people for their flocks from cards containing names of all the members. Care Corps members should report to one another at each monthly meeting regarding their work. Set up a system by which the church secretary automatically calls them when one of their group members is hospitalized or suffers bereavement. Continuing

study and discussion of one chapter a month from books that teach caring skills will provide the necessary training.
• See the Resources section for chapter 3.

10. Does our church have an organized program which helps us keep to a minimum the number of members who are inactive?

This task logically divides into two parts: One is preventive—reducing the number of persons who become inactive. The other is remedial—recovering those who became inactive several years ago.

The most productive inactive-member work is preventive. If people have a meaningful job or role in the church, if they belong to a meaningful group in the church which meets regularly, if they have several friends in the church, if they have an opportunity in the church to use the gifts God gave them in meaningful ministry, then they are not likely to become inactive. If something happens that causes them to drop out, the right kind of visit to their home within six weeks of the time that they drop out of worship can prevent 85 percent of those people from becoming inactive. The right kind of visit means a visit by a leader other than the pastor in which the right things are said and the right things are left unsaid. If, however, you wait six months before making this visit to the home of someone who drops out of worship, only 27 percent will return to activity. If you wait a year to make the visit, only 15 percent will return to activity.

These declining statistics demonstrate that the passage of time makes remedial work with inactives far less productive. This low success rate after one year however, should not prevent us from attempting to recover long-time inactive members. About every five years, we should use some organized means of encouraging people to reenter through the back door into active participation.

Action Possibilities:
• Set up a simple system to notify the pastor and key leaders when the attendance records show that a member

has three consecutive unexplained absences from worship. This enables someone to make the right kind of phone call and, if necessary, make a home visit before the close of the six-week window of opportunity during which this contact is still effective.

• Some churches have exchanged inactive-member lists with a nearby congregation of their denomination (or another denomination) and have recovered 30 percent of each other's inactive members by visiting them and inviting them to church.

The answer to each of these ten questions boils down to letting God's loving Spirit permeate our attitudes, our behaviors, our organizational systems, and our plans. An old story tells about President Thomas Jefferson making a journey on horseback with a group of friends. When they came to a swollen stream, they found a foot traveler waiting for someone to give him a ride across. The president immediately pulled him up on his horse and transported him to the other bank. "Why did you ask the president to help you across? Why didn't you ask one of the other riders?" a friend asked the man later.

"I didn't know he was the president," the man replied. "All I know is that on some faces you see a 'Yes' answer written, and on other faces you see a 'No' answer. He had a 'Yes' face."

Large numbers of members and leaders in a vital congregation have a "Yes" face.

——— IV ———
THE BEEHIVE PRINCIPLE

Honeybees have a highly developed social structure. A beehive may house as many as 80,000 bees, each of which performs a specialized duty. Some are forager bees, which fly great distances to collect food. The guard bees protect the hive entrance from intruders. The scout bees keep the hive alert to opportunities and dangers in the outside world. A few bees serve as undertakers, responsible for removing dead bodies from the hive. Others are water collectors. They bring in moisture to regulate the hive's humidity. Some are plasterers, which make a cement-like substance to repair the hive. The scent fanners station themselves at the hive entrance and blow the scent outward so that disoriented bees can locate their home base.

The Bible illustrates this "beehive principle" several times. In the Old Testament, Moses is overcome by the burdens of his office and appoints others to help him. In the New Testament, Paul says to the church at Corinth that there are varieties of gifts, varieties of service, and varieties of working, each inspired by God for the common good (I Cor. 12:5). In both I Peter 4:10 and I Corinthians 12:7, we see that these gifts are given not only to clergy. Every Christian has received gifts and has a role to play in the beehive of God's kingdom.

The leaders in a vital congregation live out this biblical principle. They recognize that God has given each of us special gifts. No Christian "has it all," but every Christian has a part of it all. Working together, they can do all God calls the church to do and be. *The pastor-people team in a vital congregation, therefore, adopts attitudes and enacts methods that involve large numbers of members in carrying out the ministry of Christ.*

The degree to which leaders succeed in involving numerous people in ministry is determined by the degree to which numerous factors are present in congregational life. Asking and answering the following questions can help leaders discover the extent to which they are practicing beehive principles.

1. Do the lay and clergy leaders in our church have a reputation for involving large numbers of people in ministry, instead of trying to do everything themselves?

Several years ago, a seminary professor and his wife were passengers on a ship bound for Europe. In the laundry room, the wife met two other women. As they talked, she learned that they were on their way to Africa to become missionaries. When she told them that her husband taught in seminary, they told her that they were graduates of that seminary. They had studied under her husband. The professor says that the insight he got from that incident was a turning point in his life. Until then, he had felt guilty about not going to the mission field. Through this experience he realized that the best way for him to do mission work was to equip others for that role. Leaders in every vital congregation have learned the same thing. They know that in order to do volumes of ministry they must resist the internal urge to do it all themselves.

To some extent, the tendency either to do it all or to ask others to help do it is an inborn personality trait. Some have it. Some do not. Delegation, organization, and the involvement of large numbers of people are, however, learnable skills. Peter Drucker, the business management guru, has said that leaders are not born and not made; they are self-taught. A self-teaching attitude is especially needed for the leadership skill necessary to involve large numbers of persons in ministry. This skill can be learned, but it must be self-taught. The first and most essential step in that direction is the recognition that this skill *must be learned* in order for a church leader to be effective in God's calling. Leaders can do a good job of massaging their own egos by allowing themselves to be trapped in the endless cycle of busyness that comes from trying to do everything themselves. But leaders cannot do a good job of helping God's church to accomplish its mission unless they learn how to get the work done by allowing other people to use their gifts in doing it.

2. Does our church focus on involving people in actual ministry, instead of merely involving them in holding church offices and serving on committees?

Thom Albin says that every church contains four types of groups. The first type engages in primary ministry. People in this group engage in the actual work for which the church was established. Evangelism calling is a primary ministry. Pastoral caring is a primary ministry. Teaching a Sunday school class and singing in the choir are primary ministries. People who are involved in a primary ministry group grow in their discipleship. The second type of group in every church focuses on *talking* about primary ministry. We usually call these groups committees. The third type of group concentrates on *talking* about people who *talk* about primary ministries. The most prominent example of that type of group is called the church board. The fourth type of group contains people who *watch* what everyone else is doing.[1]

In many churches these groups are not balanced. The fourth group, which watches, and the third group, which talks about people who talk about ministry, are equally large, but too few people engage in primary ministries. Part of the reason for this lack of balance comes from the fact, usually unrecognized by church leaders, that only about 15 percent to 30 percent of church members feel comfortable in officer

57

roles. These persons feel capable in the use of verbal skills. Most of the other 70 percent to 85 percent of persons in the group desire to serve in some way, but they feel more comfortable in *doing things* than in serving on committees where verbal skills are needed to *discuss things*. This is one of the reasons why many churches report that their best fellowship periods were (a) during a building program, (b) when the church first started and was meeting in a school, or (c) when they were holding annual bazaars or some other organized effort involving large amounts of work by large numbers of people.

Action Possibility: Each congregation should provide about sixty roles or jobs for each one hundred persons in average morning worship attendance. Eighty-five percent of these jobs or roles should involve people in doing something different from or in addition to serving on a committee that only discusses and decides things. When using that formula, count the number of jobs or roles your church has per one hundred persons in average morning worship attendance. What percentage of those jobs and roles involve actually engaging in ministry?

3. Are our lay and clergy leaders consistently giving credit and praise to people who work in our church?

Praise is like health. Few people get too much of it. Why, then, do we sometimes fail to tell people that they are doing a great job? Sometimes, we forget. Sometimes, we are too rushed and busy. Sometimes, we get too wrapped up in our own egos—which means that we are so busy looking for praise for ourselves that we do not find any for others. Sometimes, we have honestly not perceived how important praise is. We do not realize how much it helps people want to be involved and stay involved in the church's ministries. Whatever our reason for giving insufficient praise for work well done, it is not good enough. Insufficient praise in a church is like insufficient gasoline in a car. You arrive somewhere, but not where you intended.

4. Do our lay and clergy leaders continually communicate a vision of what our church needs to accomplish in the future?

Economist Adam Smith, writing two centuries ago, said that a nation's wealth is its people. That is equally true of every congregation, and the way you put your wealth to work is by continually creating a great vision. The principal religious leaders of history were people who worked at their top capacity, not just for a few minutes, but for a lifetime. They did not change the world just by working hard, however. They changed the world because they worked hard *and* shared a great vision, which inspired countless others to work hard at making the vision a reality.

5. Do our lay and clergy leaders hold their criticisms to a minimum?

A church member told his pastor that he had only one talent. "You are probably underestimating yourself," said the pastor, "but even if that is true, don't let that discourage you. What is your talent?"

"My talent is criticism," said the parishioner.

"I would advise you," said the pastor, "to do with that talent what the man who had only one talent did in Jesus' parable of the talents. Bury it."

Continual constructive evaluation is essential for the operation of an effective congregation. Personnel must be supervised. But too much criticism, instead of motivating people to want to do a better job, influences them to withdraw from doing any jobs.

6. Do we have a systematic annual program that challenges our members to consider what gifts God is calling them to use in ministry?

Bishop Richard B. Wilke says that the saddest letter he ever received was from a woman who said that she grew up in a parsonage. When she moved to a new community and joined the congregation to which she now belongs, she signed a card that asked her to volunteer. She checked greeter, usher, reader, and caller on the sick and elderly. She never heard from anyone about any of these roles. She concluded that they wanted names but not people.[2]

Many congregations do a better job of collecting volunteer cards than putting volunteers on the field. Because of insufficient attention to organization, involvement, and delegation, many of the most valuable players on their Sunday morning benches never get into the game.

Most churches have a campaign each year that asks for financial gifts. Members also need a chance to consider what spiritual gifts God has given them and how God is calling them to use those gifts. Churches involve far more people in ministry if they make the giving of time and energy a spiritual matter—instead of making it the annual ritual of trying to fill all the slots on their committees. Far too many churches use one of four negative methods to involve members in ministry: (1) arm-twisting (Would you do me a favor?); (2) guilt-tripping (If you don't do it, things will fall apart); (3) soft-soaping (But you are so good at that); or (4) slot-filling (We need six persons, and you don't have to do much). Leaders can curtail the use of these manipulative techniques by making the giving of time, energy, and talent a spiritual rather than a mechanical matter.

Action Possibility: A congregation in Brownfield, Texas, has developed an excellent process for carrying forward from year to year the responsibilities of each functional department and committee. The system has four parts—each of which is illustrated below.

About six weeks prior to the beginning of each new organizational year, the pastor preaches on the biblical theme of spiritual gifts. Such texts include: Romans 12:1-8; I Corinthians 12:1-27, 14:1-5; Ephesians 4:1-7, 11-16; and I Peter 4:8-11. During that service, he asks worshipers to indicate on a sheet the areas of church life in which they feel God has gifted them and is calling them to work this year.

One week later, the church cabinet (consisting of all committee chairpersons) meets and reviews the sheets morning worshipers completed. The cabinet may not be able to assign *every* person to the committee in which they have indicated an interest (if forty persons volunteer for the finance committee, several will need to take a second choice). After the committee lists are prepared, each chairperson calls the persons on his or her list, inviting them to serve and telling them the date and time of the first meeting. The following month all committees meet on the same night and review the responsibilities of their committee by looking at their sheet in last year's *Plan Book*. (This booklet, which the congregation publishes each year, contains the goals of each committee, church officer lists, the annual budget, the church membership list, and other housekeeping items useful to committees throughout the year.) Each committee also reviews a suggestion sheet from the pastor. It contains a list of ideas for the committee to consider in setting goals and making plans for the new year.

As a result of each committee's work, a *Plan Book* for the new year is created. It contains one sheet from each committee, describing the committee's goals and plans for the coming year. This is distributed to all committees at their next meeting—allowing members to see what each of the other committees is planning for the coming year.

7. Do we have a systematic way of helping our new members to consider what gifts God is calling them to use in the church's ministry?

A large church in Tulsa, Oklahoma, has three candlelight services each Christmas Eve. The pastor says that the church office receives several phone calls each year, asking, "Do we get to light a candle?"[3] Deep in every Christian's heart is the desire to light his or her candle.

Yet, many churches expect their new members to get actively involved in church work without any real plan for helping that to happen. Therefore, only about 30 percent of new members end up in jobs or roles for which they are spiritually gifted and psychologically suited. As a result, many of them either drop out of church or function at a very low level of productivity—which may then lead to a feeling of overload and burnout in the long-term members who desperately need help.

Action Possibility: The small congregation should train a volunteer who assumes responsibilities for new-member involvement. The large congregation, where one hundred to two hundred or more persons may join each year, needs a one-fourth or one-half-time lay staff person for this role. Whatever method you select, do not send out "Talent and Interest?" inventories in the mail. Do not leave them in the home to be returned later. Do not distribute them at a new-member dinner and expect them to be returned later. These nonproductive methods are among the most important reasons why so few members become involved in church ministries and roles.

8. Do we keep lay leadership burnout to a minimum?

One of the most destructive results of a church's failure to involve large numbers of people in ministry is the burnout of several dedicated members. Research conducted by the Alban Institute indicates that 21 percent of lay leaders in Protestant churches are suffering from burnout and another 23 percent are bordering on it.[4] This problem is like a forest fire. The bigger it gets, the bigger it is likely to get. As fewer and fewer people do more and more work, their conversations become heated with negativism rather than enthusiasm. This begins to burn off the green growth of fresh energy and creativity. A negative core of overworked leaders gives church work a burdensome reputation, rather than a fun reputation. As fewer and fewer people want to be involved, the problem intensifies. It cannot stop until (a) the forest is consumed and the church closes, or (b) a heavy rain of new leadership puts out the fire that is causing the burnout.

9. Do we have sufficient clergy and part-time or full-time lay staff members for a congregation of our size?

Increasing the number of paid staff members does not automatically increase the number of members involved in ministry. The ability of the staff, as well as their number, determines the number of volunteers involved. Insufficient paid staff does, however, automatically curtail the number of members involved in ministry. You cannot carry two gallons of water in a one-gallon bucket. This is one of the most frequently observed (yet low-profile) reasons for low member involvement in mid-sized and large churches.

One full-time pastor and a full-time church secretary can lead a church whose average morning worship attendance is in the range of 150 to 200. The older the median age of the members, the closer to 150 that ratio runs; the younger the median age of the members, the closer to 200 members in this ratio. (The older the median age, the higher the volume of pastoral work like hospitalizations and funerals.) For each additional 100 persons in average worship attendance, a church needs another paid staff person or the equivalent in part-time staff persons. When the ratio is not balanced you are courting several disastrous results: Staff members burn out; the church's ministry effectiveness is reduced; and low involvement levels among church members are experienced.

Action Possibility: Many mid-sized churches that cannot afford to add another pastor are finding it beneficial to add quarter-time or half-time lay staff persons to fill specialized leadership roles. Many larger congregations find that one to three part-time lay staff members can accomplish far more at substantially less cost than an ordained associate minister. If your church considers this approach, then the following factors are important:

a) Although it is possible to hire your own church members for these roles, be cautious. The smaller the congregation, the more often this leads to problems. As with employing relatives in the secular world, church members are easy to hire and hard to fire. People who cannot be discharged without creating chaos in the church cannot be held accountable for their job performance. The larger the congregation, the less emotional risk involved in hiring church members.

b) The system should include a ninety-day evaluation and a one-year-at-a-time contract. This allows for rethinking and renegotiation of the job description by both parties. If a staff member does not fit well with the role after a year, termination is less painful. Job description adjustments due to the church's growth or changes in other staff members can more easily be made if you have a routine, annual contract review.

c) A written job description reduces the possibility of misunderstanding and creates a base for accountability.

10. Do we have a significant number of youth or children's choirs and musical groups?

Another hidden reason for low member involvement is low involvement by children and youth. Participation by children and youth does not automatically involve their parents in church life, but it definitely correlates with and encourages parental involvement. For maximum child and youth involvement, every congregation needs two musical groups for every 100 persons in average morning worship attendance. With 100 worshipers, that usually means one adult choir and one youth or children's choir. With 200 in morning worship, that usually means one adult choir, one handbell choir, one youth choir, and one children's choir. Even in much larger churches, this ratio needs to be about the same. When children and youth get involved in a musical group, they shift from the role of being served to the role of serving others. This service inevitably deepens the sense of meaning they obtain from church participation. In most cases, their involvement produces the secondary benefit of influencing other family members to greater attendance and involvement.

11. Do the decision-making bodies of our church—the board and departments and committees—tend to encourage rather than discourage the involvement of numerous people?

Members of small congregations often complain that their church board meetings repeat the work of the committees—thus making the people who serve on committees feel that they are wasting their time. Another frequently heard complaint in small churches is the pattern of one or two leaders who bypass the normal system of board, cabinet, and committees. Still another frequent complaint among small church leaders relates to the officer and committee system recommended by their denomination: It seems to fit large congregations better than small ones. At the other end of the size spectrum, members of large congregations often complain that the board is too large. It totals seventy or eighty persons, but less than 50 percent attend board meetings.

These complaints and others like them usually stem from organizational systems that either are inappropriate to the size of that congregation or fit the thinking processes of an earlier generation but not this one. Whatever the cause of malfunction in the decision-making process of a church, leaders are more apt to fix it if they remember two things: (1) The fault is much more likely to lie in the organizational system being used than in the people who are trying to use the system. (2) The decision-making process in the church definitely influences, for better or worse, the levels of ministry involvement in the membership.

Action Possibilities:

• Congregations that are frustrated with their decision-making processes will usually benefit from (a) making certain that their board sends unresolved issues back to committees instead of trying to handle them in the board meeting, (b) making certain that all their board decisions have first been studied and recommended by a committee instead of arising from within the board or coming from one individual, (c) being certain that the board meets monthly rather than quarterly, (d) being certain that church members are not permitted to serve on more than one committee, (e) being certain that all important decisions, like a building program, are not voted on at the board meeting at which they are discussed the first time, (f) reducing the size of the board to between twelve and twenty-four members, and (g) increasing the emphasis on study, discussion, and decision making by the committees that report to the board.

• Churches that are not sure what is causing their

frustration related to organizational and decision-making processes can find out by asking all board members at one of the regular board meetings to write in one sentence on a piece of paper what they think is the primary cause of the problem (tell them *not* to sign their names). Be prepared to appoint a study committee to recommend structural changes in your decision-making processes in accordance with the consensus of opinions expressed.

12. Do our church committee meetings operate in a way that encourages rather than discourages the involvement of large numbers of people?

Committees and committee meetings have a bad reputation that they do not deserve. Contrary to popular cliches, they are not inherently boring, long, unproductive time wasters. The real culprit is insufficient training for the people who chair committees and committee meetings. Without proper skill, a bad reputation will inevitably develop regarding the committee meetings that good people lead. Airplanes do not fly without fuel. Cars do not travel without wheels. Committees do not run well without effective leadership methods.

13. Does our church newsletter communicate information in ways that encourage involvement and participation?

Leadership comes from a combination of communication and inspiration. If we try to lead by inspiration only—without adequate communication—the result is inspired confusion. If we try to lead by communication only—without adequate inspiration—the result is uninspired boredom.

The most common communication problem in small churches is no communication. Newsletters are nonexistent or insufficient in frequency. Very few churches with an average of more than 100 in morning worship attendance achieve adequate communication without a weekly newsletter.

The most common communication problem in larger

churches is poor communication. Many weekly church newsletters are weakly written, or have such a murky format and appearance that they are poorly read. Communication, like romance, requires two participants. Someone must send, and someone must receive what is sent. Many churches are sending written communication without being aware that much of it is not received. People cannot take action on what they do not know. They cannot know what they did not read because they found it too boring or too buried in too many pages of dense type.

14. Do we allow members to select the aspects of church life that are meaningful to them, instead of expecting them to show up for every meeting or event?

Leaders in small churches who expect every member to attend everything that happens in the church sometimes scold people who do not conform to this perception. This psychological sandpapering is one of the reasons many small churches stay small. Even the tiniest congregation consists of several smaller groups of people with differing interests and needs. These different types of people derive benefit from different phases of church life. Some females love women's groups; others cannot stand them but will gladly teach a Sunday school class or sing in the choir. The same variation of interests and needs is true for men. In vital, growing congregations of every size, leaders organize the programming, groups, classes, and activities as a buffet rather than as a one-dish meal. And they refrain from pointing an accusing finger at patrons who refuse to spoon up every dish in the serving line. This tolerant attitude has become far more essential in recent years. Young adults in this generation insist on options rather than uniformity.

15. Do our leaders usually exhibit a willingness to experiment with programs that are suggested by members?

Lobsters are extraordinary creatures. They run backward, smell with their antennae, taste with their feet, and chew food with "teeth" in their stomach. Predators that try to make dinner out of lobsters seldom succeed. A full suit of overlapping armor protects them. Among the world's various types of organizations, churches are about as resistant to destruction as a lobster. Unfortunately, the very armor that helps churches survive also protects them from constructive change.

Leaders of vital congregations possess a creative combination of personality traits that both conserve the institution and encourage change in it. They are willing to take off the armor and examine new ideas. This attitude is a radical contrast to the attitude of leaders of churches that resist innovation. Pastors and leaders of vital, growing churches who receive a suggestion about a new program tend to say, "Why not?" When leaders of declining churches hear a new idea, they tend to respond with statements like, "Why? We already have a lot going on." "That might conflict with what the so-and-so class is doing," or "We can't afford that!" or "Why should we do that?"

Is the person who has a new idea willing to give leadership to it? Are three or four other persons interested in the idea? If so, why not let them experiment? Unless it is illegal, immoral, fattening, or dangerous to their health, why not try it and see what happens? At least 40 percent of all new church programs fail and disappear into the sunset, no matter who thinks them up or how well they are organized. An experienced leader can spot some of that 40 percent of failures in advance. It is impossible, however, to identify all of them in their sunrise. So, why not say, "Why not?" to new program ideas?

16. Do our leaders usually exhibit an openness to discussion and disagreement?

All social systems must provide a means for the expression of differing opinions. Restrict these from coming out in meetings and they go underground—into the private world of thought and gossip channels in the parking lot and on the telephone. If restrained in public ways, contrary viewpoints often change to hostility. Many of these eventually explode in some extremely public way—like the Spanish Civil War, the Watts riots, or a taxpayer revolt. Damming up the opinion flow seldom eliminates disagreements; it usually only lengthens them. Effective leaders encourage feelings to come out in meetings and, thus, avoid having to face them later in some dark alley.

The government of New Zealand has made excellent use of its rivers for generating electrical power. One of those powerful rivers, the Waitaki, pours out of the McKenzie Basin in Southeastern New Zealand on its way to the Pacific Ocean. As it makes that long trip, the Waitaki water goes through eighteen power stations. In each one, it generates electricity used all over New Zealand.

A tourist who heard that story in a tour guide's speech responded with this question, "But isn't the power all gone out of the water before it gets to the last power station?"

No congregation generates its own energy. Its primary power source is a gift of God's Holy Spirit. But the more hydroelectric stations you build on a river, the more electricity you can produce. Leaders of vital congregations know that the more people they involve, the more ministry they accomplish.

V

LOADING THE PLANE

A Caribbean airline, now defunct, had a reputation for leaving the luggage behind. One day, people in the airport watched the plane unload luggage and then reload for its return flight. When all was secure, the plane's engines revved up, ready to taxi. Suddenly a man rushed out of the airport, frantically waving his arms, gesturing to the pilot to cut the motors. The pilot slid his window back and leaned out the cockpit window. "What's wrong?" he yelled.

The man screamed back, "The passengers—you forgot the passengers!" Congregations have numerous important ministry functions. They need to do many different things well. One of these functions, however, provides personnel for accomplishing all the others. If a church forgets to load the passengers—if people do not form an initial connection with Jesus Christ—all the other ministries will eventually stop happening. God depends on people to get most of God's good work done. No Christian people—no Christian service. No evangelism—no missions accomplished. *The pastor-people ministry team in a vital congregation therefore adopts attitudes and enacts methods that encourage people outside the church to experience a life-changing connection with Jesus Christ.*

In reaching out beyond its walls, the vital congregation is living out the words and actions of Christ. Churches in the

Western world have made faith in Christ personal (which is important), but they have also made it private. This is unbiblical and contrary to the explicit teaching of Christ.[1] According to the traditions we have in the Gospels, among the first words Jesus spoke to his disciples were, "Follow me and I will make you become fishers of men" (Mark 1:17). Three years later, the last words of Jesus, heard by his disciples, were similar: "You shall be my witnesses in Jerusalem and in all Judea and Samaria and to the end of the earth" (Acts 1:8). Between these two bookend statements of his life, Jesus traveled to the towns and villages throughout his country. On those journeys, he did what he had told his disciples to do. He pointed people toward a connection with God. During those years, his disciples heard: "You are the salt of the earth" (Matt. 5:13). "You are the light of the world" (Matt. 5:14). "The harvest is plentiful" (Matt. 9:37). "Go therefore and make disciples" (Matt. 28:19). Because of those words which we hear from Jesus, one of the symbols of office, which the Catholic church gives each new pope, is the fisherman's ring. It constantly reminds him of the primary purpose of the church. John Wesley was speaking from Jesus' worldview when he wrote, "I have one point in view—to promote so far as I am able, vital practical religion; and by the grace of God to beget, preserve, and increase the life of God in the souls of men."[2]

Each of us has an enormous need to connect with God. If we decide to do that, we gain a new, positive self-image and a new future. And yet, we are not likely to consider this powerful possibility automatically, without assistance. Someone must put up a signpost to point us in that direction. When a Sunday school teacher asked a little boy why he believed in God, he said, "I think it runs in the family."[3] Connecting with God does seem to grow in some family trees more than in others, but the trait is not genetic. We are not preprogrammed, predetermined creatures. Even Jesus' closest disciples had to be influenced to move in his direction. Jesus said to some of them, "Follow me" (Mark 1:17). Others, like Andrew, connected with Christ after John the Baptist suggested it. Simon Peter became a Christian after Andrew took him to Jesus.

Most Christians believe that religious faith gives people richer, fuller lives. They agree that encouraging people to connect with God is an important part of their congregation's mission. What they do not so readily agree upon is how to go about that. Drop the "how-to-do-it question" into the conversation of a church group, and it often explodes like a handful of firecrackers. People respond with statements like, "I certainly don't think we should do it *that way.*"

Some of these arguments contain more heat than light. For example, during the last three decades, many church leaders have been saying that congregations should engage in evangelism through the compassion of improving social structures and by writing new laws. One of every congregation's important responsibilities is influencing for the common good the social and political structures of society, but genuine evangelism rarely happens by that means. Trying to accomplish evangelism through the corporate structures of society without simultaneously doing it individually is like repairing an airplane engine and failing to teach the pilot how to fly the plane.

Fortunately, we now know more about the most effective means of encouraging individuals to connect with God than ever before in history. About two decades ago, social scientists began applying scientific research methods to the question of why some churches grow numerically and other churches do not. Congregations that apply the information derived from this research are getting the same kind of results that we see in the growth of New Testament churches. They are influencing people to connect with God in significant numbers.

Divided into its most basic (to be sure, oversimplified) elements, congregational evangelism methods involve three clear-cut parts: First, evangelization involves getting people to attend worship the first time (few people join a church until they have attended it at least once). Second, evangelization involves getting people to return to worship a second and third time (the decision to return is very different from the decision to visit once). Third, evangelization involves getting people involved with Christ and the church (birth without growth is living death). We often say, "Two out of three ain't bad." In this case, however, two out of three is terrible. All three must happen if new people are to connect with Christ in significant numbers.

The degree to which a congregation succeeds at these three elements is determined by the degree to which leaders can answer the following questions in the affirmative.

1. Do our leaders believe that we should be working hard at evangelism, even if our church does not need to grow larger for financial or other pragmatic reasons?

T. S. Eliot's lines from *Murder in the Cathedral* can easily apply to the motivational base for evangelism:

> The last temptation is the greatest treason
> To do the right deed for the wrong reason.

A pastor in a middle-sized, affluent congregation said, "We have a lot of turnover from the military base, but our membership holds about even each year. Why would we want to do an evangelism program?" He was obviously contemplating evangelism from an inappropriate motivational base. Paul says, "So we are ambassadors for Christ, God making his appeal through us" (II Cor. 5:20). People in our community have deep needs that Jesus Christ can meet. God empowers us with the Spirit when we act as his ambassadors. Whether we choose to use that power to meet those needs cannot appropriately be decided by whether our church needs the money or by the emptiness of our pews.

Relatives of American MIAs dropped 2,500 leaflets in plastic packets into the Mekong River, 700 miles from its outlet into the sea. The sheets offered a $2.4 million reward to persons in Laos, Cambodia, or Vietnam who would defect and bring American POWs out of Indochina with them.[4] Church leaders want to help others connect with Christ for the same reason—not as a selfish way to build up the organization, but as a selfless way of helping people held

73

captive by sinister forces, which make them less human than they can be.

Jesus said, "Follow me and I will make you become fishers of men" (Mark 1:17). If we are not actively engaged in this kind of fishing, then we may need to ask ourselves who or what we are following. It may be something other than Jesus. Churches that lack evangelism motivation may not need a new evangelism program so much as they need more biblical Christianity. Evangelism efforts are as natural a result of biblical Christianity as apples are a result of apple trees.

In Charles Lamb's "Dissertation on Roast Pig," the hero discovered how delicious roast pork was when his house burned down with a pig inside. He shrewdly put two and two together. Every time he wanted roast pig, he burned his house down. Increasing our evangelism efforts because of numerical membership declines in our denomination or congregation works from a similar faulty logic. Congregations that follow Jesus Christ do not need ecclesiastical disaster reports in order to become energetic in evangelism.

2. Do most of the leaders in our church want it to grow larger?

Mel Brooks tells the story of entering a delicatessen one day to buy a six-pack of beer. Upon noticing a large section of shelving filled with boxes of salt, he asked the grocer, "Do you really sell so much salt?"

"No," the man said, "I sell maybe two boxes a month. I'm, not a good salt seller. But the guy who sells me salt—he's a good salt seller!"

Many Christian leaders believe generally in evangelization, but not in specific application. Virtually all church leaders want more people to receive the benefits of connecting with Christ. An opinion poll of more than twenty-four million Protestants reveals that persuading persons to connect with Christ is number one on the list of more than a dozen things the average church member thinks a local church should do.[5] And yet, most church leaders tend to resist the changes they need to make in their congregation in order for evangelization to happen. Effective evangelism begins in exactly the same way our personal accomplishments begin. If someone decides to seek a new job or earn a college degree, that person always *begins* with an inner attitude. Evangelization *begins* when church leaders say, "Yes, we want God to use our congregation as an instrument of evangelism. We want our church to achieve a higher purpose than merely serving its own members. We want our church to serve the people who have not yet joined it. And we are willing to pay the prices involved in letting that happen."

3. Do our leaders work to keep at a minimum the blocks and inhibitors that prevent evangelism and congregational growth?

Every congregation has growth barriers. Some stem from subconscious negative attitudes, such as, "We don't want to take the time to get acquainted with and learn the names of new people who visit our worship service." Other barriers to growth can stem from the church property. If, for example, we do not have sufficient parking spaces for the worship service, that will inhibit our efforts to evangelize. Still other barriers to growth can stem from continually changing the times of services. Some churches that are linked with others on the same preaching circuit have worship at 8:30 A.M. in the summer and at 11:00 A.M. in the winter. Although this varying routine promotes a sense of equality, it also means that the public never knows what time church is. Moving targets are harder to hit. Other barriers to growth can stem from our community environment. If, for example, the population of our town begins to shrink or the type of people who live in our part of town begins to change radically, that can inhibit our efforts to grow.

Leaders of congregations effective in evangelism know that they can never completely eliminate all the growth inhibitors in their church, but they are constantly aware of and working at that task. Evangelism is to a congregation what the use of weight lifting, aerobics, and calisthenics is to an athlete—a body builder for the Body of Christ. Whatever blocks that, blocks the future God has in mind for this body and what it can accomplish together as a group of disciplined Christians.

4. Do we put as much effort into making disciples as we do into serving disciples?

Many churches operate like a factory whose goal is to manufacture personal Christian growth—while forgetting that this process cannot *begin* without new persons. Making people more Christian and making more people Christian are as distinctively different as are the medical practices of obstetrics and pediatrics. Both are necessary aspects of health care, but neither can substitute for the other. Pastors and lay leaders of growing churches give leadership to both making and serving disciples, without assuming that either is a by-product of or a substitute for the other.

5. Do the leaders in our church try to make certain that it has high visibility in the community?

Churches are not in the public relations business; they are in the business of serving people. But churches cannot serve people if people do not know they exist. Community visibility happens in numerous ways. It happens when the church building is located on a heavily traveled street. It happens when the church sign is easy to see and read from both directions. It happens when the church sign is lighted at night. It happens when the telephone *Yellow Page* ad tells what time the worship service begins. It happens when the church frequently submits articles to the local newspaper. It happens when the church advertises in the newspaper. It happens when a church uses sixty-second radio spots.

When a large percentage of the people in a community know the name of the pastor and where the church is located, you know that you have community visibility. When a stranger in town stops to ask directions to the church three blocks from the church, and the filling station attendant has never heard of it, you know that you do not have community visibility.

Chewing gum magnate William Wrigley attributed much of his success to advertising. While traveling on a fast train shortly before his death, he was asked by a friend why he continued to spend millions of dollars on advertising. Wrigley replied with another question: "How fast is this train going?"

"About sixty miles an hour, I guess," the friend replied. "Then, why doesn't the railway company remove the engine and let the train run on its own momentum?" asked Wrigley.

High community visibility is not everything in a church's evangelism efforts, but it is something—usually, something far greater than its key leaders have suspected.

Action Possibilities:

• Appoint a community visibility committee. The following checklist can help them get started.

_____ The sign in front of our church presents a well-kept appearance.

_____ The sign in front of our church is easy to see and read from both directions.

_____ The sign in front of our church is lighted at night.

_____ In addition to the sign in front of our church, we have enough other signs to let people who approach our building from other directions know we are here.

_____ Our church has additional signs on streets and roads distant from the building, which let the public know about our existence and location.

_____ Our church spends at least 5 percent of its budget a year on radio spots, T.V. spots, newspaper ads, mass mail, or *Yellow Page* ads.

_____ Our church's *Yellow Page* ad is at least three lines and contains the times of our morning worship services.

_____ A designated member or church staff person is responsible for raising questions each week with the pastor or pastors regarding items we should submit for publication in the local paper, and for submitting these articles after they are written.

● Many people feel that their denomination presents an unclear identity. To help solve that problem, one leader has suggested that a church needs to come up with a series of "one-liners" by which the members describe their congregation. For example, "We are a church that invites people to worship with their minds as well as their hearts." Have your church board or some other appropriate group write on a flip chart all the one-line descriptions they can think of that describe the stance and style of your congregation and denomination. Consider making this the motto by which you communicate your congregational identity in the *Yellow Pages* and other places.

6. Do we frequently try to motivate our members to invite their friends and acquaintances to visit our worship services?

A national study indicates that 77.6 percent of all new church members attend worship the first time because someone who attends there invites them. Personal witnessing and inviting are different. Less than 10 percent of church members feel comfortable in personal witnessing, but all church members can invite. A layman in a fast-growing church in a small town suggests this method for inviting people: At an appropriate and natural point in the conversation, say something like, "Do you folks regularly attend a local church?" Either they do or they do not. If they do, you will have an interesting conversation about church. If they do not, you can say something like, "I would really like to invite you to visit our church." Then, you tell them the address and the time of the service.

Part of the reason for the increasing effectiveness of inviting in America is the increasing responsiveness of unchurched people. The Gallup organization conducted two identical studies—one in 1978 and one in 1988. George Gallup's summary of these studies says,

> The Church, or organized religion, continues to generate greater confidence among the public than any other key institution of U.S. society. The unchurched today are, by many measures, more religious than they were a decade ago.

Almost two-thirds (58 percent) of the unchurched say they
will definitely, probably, or possibly return to church, up
from 52 percent who said that in 1978.[6]

Approximately 50 percent of the people in most communities do not attend church. If church members doubled or
tripled the number of invitations they extend each month,
the number of people who join their church each year would
significantly increase.

Someone said he asked his grandmother, age 89, how
many descendants she had. "Sixty-two," she answered.
"How did you raise them all?" he asked with a chuckle.
"I didn't raise them all, thank goodness," she replied. "I
just raised six of them. I helped some on the grandchildren.
But, I didn't do much on the thirty-five great-grandchildren
or the two great-great-grandchildren. Their parents handled
that."[7]

The idea that the pastor needs to raise all the church's
descendants is one of the most erroneous of Christian
theories. As someone has said, "Shepherds do not beget
sheep. Sheep beget sheep." That process begins through
simple invitations to worship.

7. Do our members put significant effort into building bridges of friendly relationships with worship visitors?

No amount of inviting or advertising can help a congregation if the members do not care enough to reach out in
friendly, accepting ways to visitors at worship service. In
Jesus' parable about the sheep and the goats, he ranks the
needs of strangers beside the needs of the hungry, the
thirsty, the prisoners, and the sick. "I was a stranger and you
welcomed me," he says (Matt. 25:35). Leaders need to keep
asking themselves, "Is each of us welcoming persons in our
congregation's worship service?"

Someone pointed out a huge building in downtown
Boston. She told the tourist that it is considered an
architectural marvel. Built in the shape of the state of

Massachusetts, the building has countless stairways, recesses, and alcoves. Tragically, the builders ran out of money before they finished it. On the west end of the building, two of the ornate winding stairways from the second floor end in the air twelve feet off the ground. Their steel reinforcing rods protrude from the concrete casings like the fingers of a giant comb. The building has stood there for several years, partly occupied by offices and partly uncompleted—the monument to an unfinished dream—a beautiful building with interrupted stairways leading nowhere. Friendliness between members and visitors is a stairway to a connection with Christ. If these stairways are not built by the members, most of them will remain eternally unconstructed, and visitors will not become members.

8. Does the interior of our building invite people to come back?

The silent statement that the worship area makes can be louder than the words of a friendly greeter at the front door. What does our sanctuary say? Does its atmosphere say museum, mausoleum, or festive celebration center? On the other hand, don't forget why noted church consultant Lyle Schaller says that the three most important facilities in a church, in order of importance, are (1) the nursery, (2) the women's rest room, and (3) the sanctuary. Small children tend to tell strangers how the family operates behind closed doors. Our church building tells strangers how much we really care about God's work, God's house, and the people who visit God there.

9. Do we have a coffee fellowship time immediately after worship?

When visitors have the opportunity to get acquainted with a few people, they are far more likely to return the following week. Ask greeters to serve after worship as well as before. Teach them to invite visitors to stay for the coffee moments.

Ask members to invite the strangers in the pews near them. Remind everyone that the serving should begin when the service ends. One of the best forms of serving is helping people connect with God. Helping them connect with God's loving family is an important step in that direction.

10. Do we have a system by which a layperson visits the home of all first-time worship visitors within thirty-six hours?

Information from across the United States indicates that the following formula is highly accurate:

a) If we visit the home of first-time worship visitors within 36 hours, 85 percent of them will come back next week.

b) If we visit the home of first-time worship visitors within 72 hours, 60 percent of them will come back next week.

c) If we wait seven days before visiting the home, only 15 percent of them will come back the following week.

d) If we send a clergyperson to visit the home rather than a layperson, we cut these results in half.

e) Telephone contacts instead of personal contacts usually reduce the results by at least three-fourths.

What happens in these home visits? Four things: (1) The caller says, "It was great to have you in church." (2) The caller gets acquainted with the visitor. (3) The caller answers any questions the visitor has about the church. (4) The caller invites the visitor to return next week.

Why are these immediate visits to homes so successful, and thus, so important to effective evangelization? That question has several answers, but among the most important is the church-shopper or consumer syndrome that we are dealing with in this generation. Many of the people who visit our services intend to visit several other churches before they settle on a church home. An immediate, friendly, caring visit to the home of these shoppers influences many of them to come back to our church next week instead of visiting a different one. It short-circuits their nonstop shopping intentions.

81

11. *Do we have an effective system for obtaining the names and addresses of first-time worship visitors?*

We cannot visit first-time worshipers if we do not know their names and addresses. A guest register in the narthex seldom gets signed by *everyone*, except perhaps in the tiniest of congregations (and then only if one member always comes early and devotes his or her life to getting every visitor to sign it). Using visitor cards in the pew racks or in the worship bulletins also fails to obtain a large percentage of the names and addresses of our worship attenders.

The best solution is a "Ritual of Friendship" pad in the pews. The worship leader should ask people to pass this along the pew and send it back the other direction when it reaches the end of the pew. He or she says to the congregation that this pad allows church members to learn the names of individuals who are worshiping with them. If this process is described as a friendly behavior, far larger numbers of people will sign it than if it is described as an institutional need.

12. *Does our pastor send a letter to first-time worshipers on Monday or Tuesday morning?*

This letter should recognize their presence, offer to be of service to them, and encourage them to return next Sunday. A handwritten postcard is fine. A typed letter, personally signed, is fine. Avoid form letters that look like form letters. Adding a personal P.S. can help mitigate that suspicion.

13. *Do we have an attractive, printed brochure that outlines the church programs and mission to first-time worship visitors and prospective members?*

You cannot afford to save money by mimeographing or photo copying this brochure. Produce it via the highest quality printing process. A saving of money on publicity materials always loses more money than it saves. In spite of our wishes to the contrary, people judge books by their covers. A church's cover is its printed material. The annual income lost because of the negative opinion of one family more than pays for the printing of a high-quality brochure. Use plenty of "people pictures" and concise descriptions of your program, staff, and church beliefs. On the back, print a map showing the church's location. Include the worship and church school times, the street address, and the telephone number.

14. Do we have an organized system for asking prospective members to connect with Christ or to seek church membership at the appropriate time?

People who begin attending a church and plan, eventually, to join, usually wait for someone to ask them for a decision. What if someone does not ask them to attend an information class or to make a decision regarding confession of faith or transfer of membership? A small percentage will join anyway. A few will keep attending but never join. Most, however, will eventually stop attending and disappear.

Why do church members fail to ask? Often, because they do not want to appear pushy. But the prospective member usually receives from this silence a negative message: "We don't need or want you." Most normal human beings are more inclined to procrastinate than to decide. If we want people to connect with Christ, we usually have to ask them.

An urban church, like so many in city centers, had begun to deteriorate. The water had apparently penetrated the narthex roof over the years, rotting the supporting structure. One day, the narthex fell through to the basement—taking with it a life-sized statue of Christ. Miraculously, the statue escaped damage. In preparation for rebuilding the narthex, a crane retrieved the heavy statue from the basement rubble. The workmen set it on the sidewalk in front of the church while preparing to repair the floor area to which they would return it. Two businessmen, who ordinarily walked by the church on their way to the downtown cafeteria for lunch, observed the statue. One pointed to it and said, "Well, it looks like all they've got left is Jesus."

The other replied, "At least they have him back out on the street where he belongs."[8]

VI

TAKING DOWN THE FENCES

A woman who raises African violets showed her pastor an exotic variety. "You have to have two of them," she said, "and you must set them close together, touching each other. Otherwise, they wilt."

Human nature is like that. A state of connection or bonding is more than a need; it is a necessity. Congregations are especially important in a society whose majority has been uprooted from the small close-knit communities of which America once consisted. The record-breaking audience shares of T.V. programs like "The Cosby Show" and "Family Ties" illustrate this hunger. Both portray characters connected by dependable relationships. Americans still seek money and status. In their hearts, however, they know that trying to find meaning through materialism is like applying car wax with sandpaper. The harder you work at it, the more the results elude you. That is one of the reasons why volunteerism and the percentage of Americans who contribute time to community service projects have increased so significantly in the past two decades. People are seeking meaningful connection with others.

Churches, although their central teachings focus on love, compassion, and community, sometimes develop blindness to the relationship building aspects of their ministry. For almost two hundred years, a small congregation had been five miles out of town. Its worship attendance remained about the same through the parade of each passing decade. Then the small town started growing. A new highway was completed. People now found coming here to worship as convenient as driving across town. The little church began having numerous visitors. Young couples from the new housing development on this edge of town began joining. This unexpected blessing brought with it an unexpected problem. Since leaders in this congregation had never experienced this problem before, several years passed before they recognized it.

Susan Martin said after her first year as a member, "This congregation will let you into the building, but they won't let you into the fellowship." Jim Tanner said, "They will let you into the membership, but they will not let you into the church." Ken Branson, a young businessman, asked at a Sunday school party, "How do you get on a committee in this church? Just about everyone who runs things around here either came over on the Mayflower or is the granddaughter of someone who did."

Another new member replied, "Believe me, it doesn't matter. I was appointed to a committee—probably because I am married to one of those granddaughters. We moved back to town after college. But making any significant change in this church is about as likely as your chance of persuading the president to change political parties."

Assimilation difficulties come in many shapes and forms, and they are not limited to small churches. Some large churches experience assimilation failure. To make things worse, several of the many forms of assimilation difficulty are hard to see. Church leaders are often the last to notice them. A woman in a fast-growing urban congregation said, "It is o.k. for all these new people to join. We are glad to have them. Just so they remember that it is our church, not theirs." One year later her church stopped growing because too many leaders resisted participation by the new members.

"Closing the back door" is one of the most overly discussed, underaddressed aspects of church life. Many leaders deplore results of the problem without noticing how their behavior produces it. A government panel in 1978 revealed that overexposure to the sun's rays can cause skin cancer, premature aging, and wrinkled, tough, damaged skin. Yet, a 1988 scientifically conducted poll revealed that 38 percent of women aged twenty-five to thirty-five spent at least as much time in the sun as they did five years before. Only 16 percent said they rarely spent time in the sun for beauty enhancement purposes.[1] We often observe a similar failure of a clear truth to produce changed behavior in church leaders. Even when they know that a failure to meet the connection needs of new members will increase the back door traffic, church leaders do not always pursue remedies for this danger.

The New Testament book of Acts tells the story of rapidly growing congregations. Luke repeatedly uses phrases like "added to the church" to describe that growth. Again and again, he cites the total number of new people who believe in Christ, along with the words, "and there were added to the church that day." Luke's words can help us face a crucial question: Are the people who join our congregation being added to the church, or are they just being added to the membership role?

The pastor-people ministry team in a vital congregation adopts attitudes and enacts methods that enthusiastically receive and assimilate new people into church life. The degree to which a congregation meets the need for connectedness among new members is determined by the degree to which leaders can say yes to the following questions.

1. Do most of our members and leaders exhibit an attitudinal openness toward newcomers?

Some churches are surrounded by invisible glass walls (invisible to their long-time members, but everyone else can see them clearly). They are friendly people—but generally toward each other more than toward others. They are one big happy family—but a family that doesn't grow bigger, merely older. For example, a farming area gradually merged with a suburban bedroom community. The conservativeness and clannishness of long-term members caused them to over-look, ignore, and actually fear the newcomer group. And the same thing happens in some city churches.

In an interview with Bill Moyers, Joseph Campbell pointed out that brotherhood is usually confined to a bounded community. One of the Ten Commandments told the Israelites not to kill. The next chapter of Exodus instructs them to invade Canaan and kill everyone in it. The values that instructed the behaviors of their pre-monarchic culture recommended love for the in-group and aggression toward those outside the bounded community.[2] Jesus changed those values, breaking down the barriers between the in-group and the out-group. He took down the fences around the Old Testament's bounded community. Leaders in the congregations established by his disciples have not all caught up with this shift toward inclusiveness.

A city planner says that we must find ways to create within the urban environment a sense of belonging. Churches, when operating according to their designer's blueprint, are one of the finest ways to meet this need. This atmosphere, however, does not come into being without conscious effort. Leaders must continually point long-term members toward an attitude of openness toward newcomers. Otherwise, they slip back to in-group, exclusive behavior as naturally as a heated home grows cold when the furnace fails.

Action Possibilities:

• If your church has not published a pictorial directory of members within the past three years, consider doing so. New members find it difficult to feel included in a place where they have trouble putting the names and faces together. Call the appropriate department within your denominational head-quarters for a recommendation of companies that excel at this type of work.

• Give the names of new members to the leaders of Sunday school classes, youth groups, women's groups, athletics teams, and men's groups so that they can seek to involve them.

• Ask lay leaders to make welcome calls and get-acquainted calls on all new members within two weeks after they join.

2. Do our members exhibit appealing personalities?

A few members in every congregation are set in their ways, stingy, suspicious, and clannish. When numerous members in a congregation share that pattern, the church is unattractive to both newcomers and long-term residents. Birds of a feather flock together, and hummingbirds are not attracted to a flock of pelicans. Since individual personality is highly resistant to reconstruction, this is one of the toughest kinds of congregations to help. Some small churches stay locked in a neutral gear for decades owing to this syndrome. This problem is usually resolved in one of two ways: One is a series of funerals. The other is a huge influx of new members who dilute the pervasiveness of negative personalities.

3. Do we exhibit an attitude of high expectation regarding the contribution new members will make to congregational life?

In a frequently cited research study, public-school teachers were unknowingly given falsified records about their students. These records indicated that their students of average ability had high IQ scores. By the end of that school year, many of those average students were doing as well as the truly gifted students. The teachers' expectations had improved the performance of the students. The same self-fulfilling prophecy happens in churches. What you see is often what you get. This is especially true of what church leaders see in the potential of their new church members.

Action Possibilities:

• Never permit chairpersons to pick their committee members in isolation. Ask them to meet and review the membership list, along with information such as that obtained from a "Spiritual Gifts Commitment Sunday." Then, select potential committee members by meeting together as a team of chairpersons. This protects the chairpersons from asking some church members to serve on two committees while neglecting other people altogether.

• Organize a Sunday school teacher corps in which you have four, five, or more substitute teachers for each class.

That gives new members a feeling of doing something worthwhile for the church but does not overload them. It also strengthens the Sunday school program. Since all "master teachers" have several substitutes to call in an emergency, they never have to phone the Sunday school superintendent to find a replacement when they are sick or out of town. Under this system, the master teacher teaches during the nine months of the school year and the teacher corps members handle the three summer months.

● Write newsletter stories about new members being appointed to responsibilities.

● Introduce new members at the next fellowship dinner after they join, letting them know by letter the foregoing week that they will be introduced at that time and will be guests at this first dinner.

● Some pastors, especially in larger churches, set up a system for sending out a series of two or three personal letters to new members during the first six months or year after they join.

4. Do we tend to invite new members to serve on church committees, rather than ask only older members, several of whom serve on more than one committee?

In both small and large churches, the pastor and officers naturally tend to pile the key leadership roles onto a few persons. This gradual centralization is a normal result of three causes: (1) We tend to ask people we know personally to help us. (2) We tend to ask people who have proved their dependability in the past to help us. (3) We tend to ask persons to help us if we know that they agree with our viewpoints. Paring down to a smaller nucleus is natural, but it tends to burn out the hardest-working core leaders. It simultaneously reduces the involvement (and thereby the commitment) of numerous other members.

5. Did 50 percent of our current officers and board members join our church in the past twelve years?

The average congregation adds enough new members each year to total at least 5 percent of its membership. This means that at least one-half of the members of the average church joined within the last ten years. Does your church's officer-and-board group reflect that percentage? If not, the leaders are probably either knowingly or unconsciously resisting the inclusion of new people and new ideas. The majority of persons who join a church are happy to *follow*, but some want to lead. If these persons do not get that chance, they fade away and find a church in which they can.

Action Possibility: Call together a group of long-term leaders. Distribute membership lists. Write beside each name all the church offices and roles each person holds. Jobs will cluster around some people. Keep this list handy during nominating committee meetings, other committee meetings, and cabinet meetings during the coming year. You can involve many of the persons who have white spaces beside their names. This procedure is especially helpful in churches where certain individuals (because of personal inclination, or by accident or great skill) are overextended in church work.

6. Do the new members of our church find it easy to make new friends within the church?

Someone said that home, in one form or another, is the great object of life. What is the item most essential for feeling at home? Friends!

Flavil Yeakley interviewed fifty active laypersons who had been members of their respective congregation for at least six months. He found that people who stayed active had acquired an average of seven or more friends in the church. Interviews with persons who had dropped out revealed that they averaged less than two new friendships.[3] The leaders of vital growing churches instinctively know the importance of friendship. So, the leaders organize to accomplish it.

Action Possibility: Involve adult Sunday school classes in the assimilation process by using the "Magic Three Plan." This will draw up to 80 percent of new adult members into Sunday school classes, thus increasing the likelihood that they will begin several friendships. In this process, each class is asked to select a recruitment officer. During the first week after each new member joins, the pastor notifies the recruitment officer for the class whose members have ages and interests similar to those of the new members. The recruitment officer makes a twenty-minute visit to the home of the new member to get acquainted, to say "We are glad you joined our church," and to invite the new member to his or her adult Sunday school class. The following week, another person or couple from the same class makes a similar visit. The third week, same play, different visitor. This organized extroversion helps new members feel wanted, while assuring the numerical health of adult classes.

7. Do we do a good job of accepting the new ideas and the changes that always come when new members assume leadership roles?

All fast-growing churches hit a crisis point at which the old guard resists the influx of new members. This resistance is natural. Rapid change in any social system breeds some confusion and frustration. Thus, the same leaders who rejoice when God adds to the church weekly, begin to grouch when rapid growth stimulates a reshaping of the organization. Most of these church leaders cannot see past their own feelings to the real root of their anxiety—resistance to change. In some cases, however, seasoned leaders will flatly state, "With all these new people, it just doesn't seem like the same church anymore. I like it the way it used to be."

Another cause of this natural resistance to growth is key leadership displacement. A year earlier, the church officers had said with great feeling, "Our church needs to grow." It did. But they didn't. What they had really meant was, "Our church needs to grow, but don't make any changes in leadership. I've grown accustomed to these faces. Make the army bigger, but don't change the officer corps."

Combating this natural resistance to change is particularly hard for the pastor. He or she would prefer that older members appreciate "what I have done to help the church grow." But the pastor always learns that numerical growth is a surprisingly two-pronged task—helping the saints to multiply and then helping them to be happy that they did.

8. Do we have an organized system designed to assist all new members within the first two months in becoming part of a class or group which meets regularly and which offers some role or responsibility within the first six months?

Some small congregations do this *too well*. They elect someone as property chairperson before he or she gets dried off from baptism. Big churches tend to the opposite extreme. Unless new members possess aggressive, outgoing personalities, they slip through the organizational cracks. People need signals of acceptance from their new church family. If they do not get these signals, many of them silently feel hurt. This lack of initial acceptance sometimes leads to hostility about some minor matter, which then becomes a pressure valve for their pain. Or, they just silently fade away to the inactive list—another way to reject being rejected.

Two things must happen to all new members if they are to stay active in the church and grow in spiritual maturity: (1) Within a month or so after joining, they must begin a relationship with some small group in the church. This could be the choir, a Sunday school class, the women's group, a men's softball team, or any of a dozen other kinds of face-to-face groups. Only then will they feel themselves a real part of the church. (2) Within three to six months, they must get involved in some kind of job or responsibility in the church. If these two needs are not met, one year later, 80 percent of new members will no longer be regular worship attenders.

In church life, just as in family life, nothing substitutes for a sense of belonging. Great preaching cannot substitute for it. Beautiful buildings cannot substitute for it. If we expect people to feel a sense of belonging by accident, many of them will not. If we systematically work at providing love, inclusion, and opportunities for healthy interaction, most of them will.

Are you doing that in your church?

—— VII ——
PUTTING THE WHEELS ON

The horse was laboring hard to pull a Maine farmer's wagon along a country road. As they passed a man cutting weeds by the roadside, the farmer asked how much longer the hill lasted. "Hill?" said the man with the scythe. "There is no hill. Your back wheels have come off."

The much publicized membership shrinkage in many mainline denominations stems from a similar situation. Some time ago, it appeared that these churches were running uphill against a general resistance to religious institutions, which was caused by the increasing secularism of American culture. But the rapid growth of community Bible churches and denominations like the Assemblies of God during the last twenty years proves that there is no hill. Rather, mainline churches have lost their basic means of momentum. The central mainline problem is not just a resistant secularism but failure to meet the spiritual needs for which people turn to churches. The back wheels have come off.

Eighty thousand readers of *Better Homes and Gardens* responded to a questionnaire, which asked, "What do you most want from a religious organization?" Eighty percent of those eighty thousand people responded "spiritual development."[1] That survey was not based on a scientific sample, but its data are consistent with earlier scientific findings. A study published by the Princeton Religion Research Center indicated that the top priority of Christians is "concentrating on the spiritual growth of one's family and self."[2] This data also explains why the percentage of children in the United States receiving religious education grew from 60 percent in 1978 to 69 percent in 1988. This data is also consistent with statistics that show an increasing responsiveness to Christianity among young adults. Churches are growing numerically when they provide meaningful opportunities for people to grow in their understanding of the Bible and in their sense of spiritual relatedness to God through prayer.

An atheist group, the Freedom from Religion Foundation, has requested that hotels and motels in the American Hotel and Motel Association provide "Bible-free" rooms. The group says that hotels and motels offer "smoke-free" rooms; therefore, atheists should not have to accept rooms equipped with Bibles.[3] To put the matter in proportion, very few people in the United States view life from an entirely atheistic perspective. For example, one out of three adults, including those who never attend church, say they have had a powerful religious insight or awakening at some point in their lives.[4] Helping people to build on those spiritual experiences is therefore one of the central tasks of every church. This brings us to the seventh characteristic of a vital congregation: *The pastor-people ministry team in a vital congregation provides Sunday school and other small groups that offer Bible study and spiritual growth opportunities and meet many spiritual and social needs.*

What does the term "spiritual growth" mean? Well-known author Bernie Siegel defines spirituality as a state of mind that includes acceptance, faith, forgiveness, peace, and love.[5] A Catholic writer, James Finley, says that our spirituality is determined by how we image ourselves and how we image God.[6] The degree and type of spirituality we possess thus transcends the reality of our personal circumstances. Spirituality is the mental lens through which we look at and interact with the reality around us, other people, and our future. That makes our spiritual makeup far more important than our psychological makeup, our sociological circumstances, or our cultural environment. To grow spiritually means that we change the lenses of our glasses. We grow in our ability to view our environment and the purpose of our lives from God's perspective. By doing this, we experience a miracle: We change reality by transcending it. Jesus did not eliminate the reality of water. He walked on it and changed it into wine. Through spiritual growth, we do that too.

This function of a vital congregation—helping people to grow spiritually—is deeply rooted in every part of the biblical record. Teacher was the description most frequently applied to Jesus by his peers. More than thirty times, the Gospel writers record that people referred to Jesus as teacher. Again and again, we hear phrases such as, "And he opened his mouth and taught them, saying" (Matt. 5:2). When Jesus sent the disciples out to expand his effort to help people connect with God, teaching was one of the key strategies in their game plan. "Teaching them to observe all that I have commanded you" (Matt. 28:20), he said. The apostle Paul is continuing this emphasis on spiritual growth when he writes to the Ephesian church. He suggests that we should all strive to "attain to the unity of the faith and of the knowledge of the Son of God, to mature manhood, to the measure of the stature of the fulness of Christ; so that we may no longer be children, tossed to and fro and carried about with every wind of doctrine" (Eph. 4:13-14).

Vital congregations help people grow spiritually in several different ways. The degree to which churches accomplish this task is determined by the degree to which leaders can answer the following questions in the affirmative.

1. Do we have sufficient numbers and types of Sunday school classes and other kinds of groups to meet the needs of a wide variety of people?

The "insufficient programming syndrome" is more obvious when it appears in small congregations, but it can also occur in mid-sized and large congregations. When a church limits in volume and variety the basic bread-and-butter programming, such as Sunday school and Bible study for various age groups, the members see insufficient opportunities for spiritual growth. The visitors see little that inclines them toward returning.

Bible study, prayer, and relating to a group of like-minded people helps us connect with God. This is why so many young adults are interested in spiritual growth groups of various kinds. This is not the only reason why many congregations in the Assemblies of God—with their emphasis on evangelism through home cell groups—are growing so rapidly. These congregations connect disconnected people with one another and God. Many of the mega churches and Korean congregations use cell groups too. The group participation that they provide meets the deep human need to belong.

Being a "joiner" is out now, an outdated status-seeking method from the 1950s. But to "belong" is still in and always will be. To feel that you belong, really belong, is a healing, enriching medication for the psyche and your self-esteem, especially when linked to a spiritual relationship with God. Those who feel that they belong to God's family inherit something more than the Kingdom; they inherit a psychological well-being beyond anything that they can self-manufacture.

Action Possibility: Check on your church using the following formula: Count all the groups: Sunday school classes, choirs, women's groups, men's groups, cabinet, board, functional committees, and so on. Then divide the total participating church membership by the total number of groups. If your quotient is larger than sixteen, the church does not contain enough primary groups. If your church fails to measure up to this "sweet-sixteen principle," then it is short on fellowship and participation opportunities. People roll away before they ever get firmly related to the church, like apples off the top of a full basket. Ironically, the larger the church the greater the likelihood of underprogramming. The staff and leaders feel that "we are so terribly busy: this church is surely providing a very wide-ranging program!" Their own hectic schedule thus keeps them from seeing the program opportunities, which, if instituted, would mean growth for the church.

2. Do we focus primarily on the spiritual aspects of what the church is trying to do, rather than on the organizational and financial aspects that support what the church is trying to do?

Historian Paul Johnson said, "In the last resort, our civilization is what we think and believe. The externals matter, but they cannot stand if the inner convictions which originally produced them have vanished."[7] This demand for core convictions is equally and perhaps even more true of congregations and denominations. Christianity is much more than relating to a group, and more than pride in preserving a worthy cultural institution.

One researcher notes that a study of five principal denominations shows a membership decline equivalent to a 700-member congregation closing down every day for fifteen years. He claims that the main factor in this decline is the feeling among members that they are not being fed spiritually. "When churches are not on fire for their faith any more, they become vulnerable to other ideas," he adds.[8]

In some churches, both the members and those who visit begin to sense that one of the "other ideas" upon which the leaders are focusing is institutional preservation. In some cases, this begins to happen during several years of financial struggle to keep the church doors open. In trying to keep expenditures to a minimum, leaders unconsciously shift their focus from the spiritual to the materialistic. Over a long period of time, the church board loses its vision about the basic purposes of the church. When this happens, the organization becomes a "building and grounds committee," which, to outsiders, looks like a hybrid between a mausoleum and a museum. Few people are inspired to full participation by the idea of preserving an institution. They know that healthy churches focus on the spiritual rather than the material.

3. Do we concentrate primarily on involving people in study and fellowship groups, rather than focus primarily on involving them in committee work?

Imprisoned and near the end of his life, Paul requested three things: a cloak, a visit from Timothy, and some books.

Scholars are reasonably certain that the reading material was portions of Scripture. Paul was expressing the basic need of all Christians everywhere—the physical (clothing), the emotional (a loving relationship), and the spiritual (God's Word). Many churches too often provide only one or two of those three essentials for their members.

Involvement in committees is not enough. Very little spiritual growth or emotional nurture occurs in committee meetings. But most churches have a committee structure in place. This structure has personnel slots that demand filling each year. Leaders are therefore easily deluded into focusing on "involvement through committee work" rather than "involvement through study and fellowship." This misdirection is especially true in small churches, which are often pressured into using organizational charts designed for churches five times their size. This keeps the members busy running the organizational machinery. They have no time left to participate in opportunities for emotional nurture and spiritual growth, which the church's organizational machinery is supposed to provide. They are so busy greasing the mammoth machine that they have no time to manufacture anything with it.

A doctor who invented groups for cancer patients says that the groups try to accomplish what Alcoholics Anonymous tries to do for its members—sharing, acceptance of responsibility, spiritual awareness, and life-style changes.[9] Are not these the objectives of what churches should provide their members? Committees and task forces are essential to congregations, but they seldom accomplish those nurturing and spiritual objectives.

Action Possibility: If your church is small and suffers frustration from trying to use an organizational structure of committees and departments more suitable for a much larger congregation, consider shifting to a council system. Appoint the usual committee chairpersons, but instead of holding eight separate committee meetings each month, call these chairpersons together for a monthly council meeting one week prior to each board meeting. (Small churches averaging less than eighty in worship attendance may want to hold this council meeting only five times each year—September, November, January, March, and May.) At the council meetings, committee chairpersons take turns bringing up matters from their sections of church life. While each chairperson has the floor, the other chairpersons become members of the speaker's committee for those few minutes. This ensures democratic input and protects chairpersons from solo flights into ill-advised decisions. Following the council meetings, committee chairpersons ask other members of the congregation to execute specific tasks or events (such as planning the Christmas party). But each appointee's responsibility continues only for the duration of that project. Specific talent is thus used in specific ways, involving the whole membership in various activities throughout the year. Many people who refuse to serve on a committee for the entire year gladly agree to work on a specific project.

4. Do our leaders usually respond with an open, "Why not?" attitude toward people who want to start new groups?

George Gallup, Jr., says that the new interest in Bible study and prayer fellowship groups is one of the most hopeful signs in America. "People are discovering that faith grows best in the presence of faith," he says.[10] Jesus said something similar: "But you do not believe, because you do not belong to my sheep" (John 10:26).

The senior pastor of a rapidly growing United Methodist congregation in Wisconsin defines a small group this way: any group other than a committee that meets at least monthly and has a friendship or fellowship function in addition to its other purposes. The number of such groups in his church has grown from twenty-seven to eighty-one in the last eight years. Some of these groups include bell choirs, study groups at home and church, singles' groups, United Methodist Women circles, young mothers' groups, men's early morning prayer and study groups, a baseball team, and a golf group. The pastor says, "Our philosophy is, 'Where two or three persons express an interest or a need, there are others who will also be interested, and a small group will be formed.' We plan to continue adding six new small groups each year."

Small groups and classes do not, by themselves, cause growth and vitality in a congregation, but vital congregations always have them. Therefore, the only appropriate response to someone who wants to start a new group is, "Why not?"

5. Do we concentrate on developing strong adult Sunday school classes, rather than concentrate only on children and youth classes?

Children do not drive cars or make decisions about how the family spends Sunday mornings; adults do. Leaders in vital congregations therefore concentrate on drawing larger circles, which take in more adults, rather than emphasize youth and children's activities only.

6. Do our classes and groups work hard at providing an extroverted fellowship climate?

Many adult classes stay the same size for the same reason that most small churches remain static in numbers. The warmth of their fellowship locks strangers outside. "We are such a friendly group," they proudly exclaim. But to whom? Mostly to each other. To outsiders, they seem like a closed shop. Until leaders deal with this "invisible introversion," significant growth is seldom possible.

All prospective adult class members look for one thing above all others: *active acceptance.* They hope class members will care about them and want them in their social group. Adult classes that systematically provide this acceptance tend to grow. Four ingredients are particularly significant for increasing class extroversion: (1) a gregarious greeter. Always early, he or she remembers names and faces and has the social knack of making strangers feel like home folks. (2) Name tags. Every Sunday, for every class attender. This makes newcomers feel equal and reduces the social awkwardness of feeling that everyone is acquainted except you. (3) Coffee, tea, and so on, in each classroom. The coffee urn distributes more than caffeine. Everyone knows how to fix and drink a cup of coffee. This gives strangers something specific to do with their hands. (4) Occasional class social events. Invitations to picnics and parties are much more personal than invitations to attend a Sunday school class. Hence, they increase the feeling of acceptance.

7. Do we frequently start new adult classes?

Even the smallest of congregations should try to start a new adult class every five years. Mid-sized and large churches should start a new adult Sunday school class every year or two. New members are much more likely to join a class while it is being organized than one that has been meeting since 1906. Why? Because becoming part of something new has more psychological appeal than joining an established group. Because people know they will have a chance to shape the class structure and the study model in a new group. Because the leader types know it is not too late to be accepted as a leader in a new group. Because the timid types feel that they will find a secure place of acceptance in a new group. Because a new group stays "extroverted" for many months before it begins to erect the "invisible glass walls" that discourage new attenders. Because people get older, and there is a perpetual need to establish another "young married" class. Because it is easier to start a new group than to try to "change out" a teacher entrenched in outdated methods. Because very few adult classes grow to more than thirty on the roll, with fifteen to twenty regular attenders.

Anticipate some resistance from older members who have worked hard for years to make their classes grow (often without success). These saints will cry "foul!" when new study groups are formed—unless you help them to understand that new people can be reached in this way who will never attend an established class.

8. Do we have at least one group, Sunday school class, or athletic activity which is effective in attracting young adults, ages twenty to thirty-seven?

Approximately one-third of the population of the United States is in that age bracket. Yet, church committees and boards, perhaps because they are usually composed of older adults, tend to overlook programs that meet the needs of this younger age group. The pastor of a growing church in Kansas says:

> We targeted young adults as a group that we wanted to reach. We did this by starting new programs—such as athletics (which resulted in several couples coming into our church), new Sunday school classes for young adults and children, and small group Bible studies. We improved our nursery, started younger youth groups, and organized a children's choir. In short, we began to offer ministries that met *their needs* instead of just our needs. As a result, the number of young adults in our church has increased substantially.

9. Do we have a group that meets the needs of young single adults?

Not every church can develop a singles program. Because singles are hungry for social relationships, they are magnetically attracted to churches already having a large number of singles. Building a strong singles program always takes a great deal of effort anywhere, but it is much easier to do in a large church than in a small one. The large church already has a beginning nucleus. Whatever your church's size, recognize that singles come in several different types. Some singles are divorced with small children. Some singles are older, with grown children. Some singles are younger and have never been married. Some singles are college students. Churches with an effective singles program usually began it by trying to assemble a group that met the needs of the type of singles they already had in the church. Later, after the snowball began to roll up to a bigger size, they often started a group or groups for other types of singles.

10. Do we have a group or program that meets the needs of older adults?

Demographics experts tell us that the total number of Americans above the age of sixty-five will soon equal the number of persons below the age of twenty-one. This makes ministry to and through that age group increasingly important. Many of those individuals still have fifteen to twenty years of productive life expectancy after they stop their salaried employment.

11. Do we have strong Sunday evening junior-high and senior-high youth programs?

Youth programs do not automatically cause churches to grow, but growing churches tend to have strong youth programs—undoubtedly because growing churches usually contain a large number of families with children and youth. Churches that do not meet the needs of these young families do not *continue to grow*. The chief exception to this rule is churches located in retirement communities—which can grow without any youth whatsoever.

12. Does our women's organization attract large numbers of young adult women?

Church women's organizations that achieve large attendance rates usually structure themselves quite differently from those that succeeded during the 1950s. Their goals are also quite different from those of the women's organization that flourished in the fifties.

13. Do most of our Sunday school teachers and leaders work hard at increasing the size of their classes?

The 1960s brought many positive elements to Christian education work. Among these were a more professional approach in the training of Sunday school teachers and the emphasis on high-quality instruction. But these positives unintentionally perpetrated one negative. As Sunday school teachers tried to emulate models appropriated from successful public school teachers, some forgot that quality teaching does not automatically produce high attendance. Large classes, whether they are adult or children's classes, get large because someone intended for them to get large. The teacher (and other leaders) had to work intentionally at and use specific methods in order to make that happen. The quality of the teaching is always one important element in the growth of a class or group. It never by itself produces growth.

14. Do we provide adults at least one new short-term opportunity for group study each year in addition to the regular Sunday school classes?

If we intend to attract new people to group study, we must occasionally offer something different. Otherwise, a person's decision not to become involved in a class or group is likely to remain the same. A good rule is to intentionally offer one *completely new* six-week to twelve-week study for adults each year that is different from anything done before. Resist the temptation to build on one of your successes by calling it the "first annual whatever." This transforms an interesting, people-attracting innovation into a less attractive routine.

Many kinds of methods are effective in strengthening Sunday school classes and groups. These diverse programs do, however, have one element in common. They always meet the real felt needs of church members and people in the community. They do not focus on meeting the felt needs that leaders have for "doing what we have always done," "what we enjoyed doing when *we* were young adults," and "what we think young adults *ought* to want to do in the church."

Right now, young adults believe that personal spiritual growth is what churches need to provide. That cannot happen in Sunday morning worship alone. It always requires some kind of small-group involvement. Some church leaders will object to the personal growth principle. "Churches must

surely do more than merely set up spiritual cafeteria lines,"
they will say. This objection contains some truth. A vital
congregation always does much more than meet personal
spiritual needs. But it dare not do less than offer a satisfying
spiritual experience.

Elton Trueblood wisely observed long ago that faith
consists of roots and fruits. For several decades, many United
States church leaders were urging people to produce the fruit
of faith while giving little emphasis to helping them nurture
the roots of faith. Now, these leaders are rediscovering two
facts: (1) Without roots, the volume of fruit among church
members ultimately diminishes. (2) Unchurched people
respond to churches that help them grow spiritual roots.

---VIII---

THE BEST KIND OF NETWORKING

To illustrate his speech regarding the importance of networking with other leaders in your field, a college president said that he had been in Washington the preceding week. After a meeting with the vice president of the United States, he spoke briefly with the president. Then he added with a broad smile, "But that is no big deal. This morning, I talked with God! So, when you are trying to succeed by making the right connections, don't neglect your *most important* connection."

What is so obviously true for individuals is also true for congregations. Success is a matter of making the right connections—and prayer is the best way to make that right connection. Prayer opens the door that lets the mind of God into our thinking and behavior. Insights, rational thinking, and fine-tuned methods are important. But without a connection with God through prayer, our church can become an expensive solar-powered watch into which someone forgot to put the energy cell. We have a lot going for us, but it doesn't take us anywhere.

Jesus' disciples recognized this principle early in their travels with him. Luke records their insight this way: "He was praying in a certain place, and when he ceased, one of his disciples said to him, 'Lord, teach us to pray, as John taught his disciples' " (Luke 11:1). Nowhere else do we find the disciples requesting instructions for how to do something. They do not say, "Teach us how to preach." They do not say, "Tell us how to build a church." They do not even say, "Show us how to perform miracles." Why, then, this request for instruction in prayer? Jesus' prayer connection was so visibly the crux of his strength that they wanted to know how they could be empowered in the same manner.

Every renewal leader in church history echoes that conviction. John Wesley, like so many others who changed the world for God and good, rose at 4:00 A.M. to spend a lengthy time in prayer. A letter he wrote to Ellen Gretton in 1782 characterizes his convictions on this matter: "Proceed with prayer," he said, "and your way will be plain."[1]

The average person in today's society—even those who are not overtly religious—is acutely aware of this need to make the right connection. When a *Better Homes and Gardens* survey asked eighty thousand readers this question: "Faced with a spiritual dilemma, what guides you most?" sixty-eight percent of them answered "prayer/meditation."[2]

This hunger for a connection with God through prayer seems greater today than in the preceding generation. Among the several reasons behind our need for prayer is our feeling of compartmentalization in this technological age. In a world of unlimited information, each of us lives in a narrow, specialized field. No matter how well educated we are, we know that we have only a coffee cup's worth out of the Pacific Ocean of available information. More than earlier generations, we know how much we do not know.

Stress is another reason for an increased hunger for networking with God. Three out of five adult Americans say they feel under great stress at least once a week. More than one in four feels under great stress several times each week. The people most likely to feel stressed are college graduates, those with the highest income, and persons forty to forty-nine years of age.[3]

Our personal concept of God is the greatest determinant of how big our problems look to us. If we have a big God, our problems look small and distant. If we have a small God, our problems look like bull elephants heading in our direction. Prayer helps us to have a bigger God—not because God gets bigger through praying but because we move closer to God and gain security from that proximity. French and West German companies have devised techniques to use lasers in sorting and recycling garbage. The lasers can sort material by color, texture, weight, and toxicity.[4] Prayer is a spiritual laser that helps us to recycle our stresses, mistakes, and ignorance into something better.

No wonder then that *the pastor-people ministry team in a vital congregation adopts attitudes and enacts methods that teach members how to nurture a life of prayer.* This ministry fits with the reality of human need. It fits with the experience of Jesus' first disciples. It fits with the experience of every renewal leader in history. It fits with the convictions of Christians today, and even fits with the convictions of non-Christians.

How can churches help their members nurture a life of prayer? The degree to which churches accomplish this important task is determined by the degree to which leaders can say yes to three questions.

1. Do our worship services and other public functions seem to communicate a conviction about the importance of prayer?

During the Summer Olympics in Seoul, two members of the United States Diving Team decided to attend church one Sunday morning. Neither of them could speak Korean, and their taxi driver could not speak English. After numerous futile efforts at communicating their desired destination, one of the divers put his hands together in front of him to symbolize prayer. A gleam of understanding came into the taxi driver's eyes. He nodded knowingly and drove the two Americans to the city swimming pool.[5] Some observers of the American religious scene note a similar failure of some church leaders to read accurately the need of their congregation to network with God in prayer. The services place heavy emphasis on form. Worship is impersonal, providing too few opportunities for lay participation. People who are looking for the transcendent presence of God sometimes leave feeling as if they have visited the city swimming pool.

Congregations that fail to communicate a conviction about the importance of prayer are seldom aware of their problem. This ignorance usually occurs when they have subtly substituted some other important ingredient for the most important ingredient. In Holman Hunt's picture, "The Light of the World," Jesus is knocking at a door on which there is no outside latch. Someone must open it from the inside. A little boy was talking to his father about the picture. "Why don't people open the door?" he asked.

His father replied, "I guess they don't want to."

"No, I don't think that is the reason," the boy said. "I think it is because they all live in the back of the house."[6]

How very easy it is for a congregation, without knowing it, to live in the back of God's house. If our primary conviction is that psychological self-help is valuable, then we are probably communicating that to worshipers. If our primary conviction is that our particular denomination's doctrinal position is vital, then we are probably communicating that to worshipers. If our primary conviction is that connecting with God through prayer is important, then we are probably communicating this most important conviction. Does our congregation live in the back of the house, or do we open the door?

2. Do we emphasize the importance of prayer as much as we emphasize the importance of rational thinking and representative democracy?

First Korean Christian Church of Chicago had outgrown its building and was looking for a larger facility or a piece of land on which to build a new building. At one point the church was very close to closing on the purchase of a site. They were so certain of this that they sold their old building to another church. But the deal for the new site fell apart. They leased space for a short time, since they had sold their old building. After almost eight months in leased space, and when several "sure things" had fallen through, the pastor decided that the power of real estate agents was limited. The leaders turned to the power of prayer and fasting. On the first day of their forty-day prayer and fasting plan, the pastor and his family prayed all day and fasted for two meals. On the next day, one of the elders did this, and so on through the church the process went. Within a week, leaders received a phone call about a church that wanted to sell its building on Chicago's northwest side, an ideal spot. Within the forty days they had set for prayer and fasting, the building had been inspected and financing had been arranged. Shortly after completing the forty days, they closed on the property.

Churches are busy organizations. The leaders must keep committees operational, run the Christian education program, and do countless other important chores. In that flurry of activity, our primary task of helping people relate to God in prayer is easily displaced in favor of more "practical matters." Some of the churches in Africa, when they have an important decision to make, meet at dusk and pray until dawn. One cannot help wondering—is this concentration on making the right connection part of the explanation for the enormous numerical growth of African churches? Richard Halverson has said that Christianity started in Palestine as a relationship. It became an idea in Greece, an organization in Rome, and a business enterprise in America.[7] Prayer is the primary way we return it to a relationship status.

Action Possibility: Increase the warmth and caring among church officers while helping to strengthen their spiritual life. To do so, divide the church governing body into groups of four persons each who covenant to pray for one another daily. Ask these same persons to spend eight minutes together in their groups at each board meeting, sharing their experiences with one another.

3. Do we have some type of organized prayer chain or prayer tree in which all our members are involved?

A Gallup poll indicates that 87 percent of Americans pray at some time each day. That figure includes 75 percent of those who are *not* members of a church or synagogue and half of the people who subscribe to no formal religion. In the past, people who prayed tended to be the aged, the sick, the poor, and those with limited educational backgrounds. Today, a growing number of well-educated, affluent young adults find value in prayer.[8] That helps explain why young adults respond positively to prayer trees, prayer chains, prayer circles, prayer partners, and daily prayer covenants. They already believe in prayer, and therefore they appreciate the opportunity and encouragement to practice it.

A congregation launched in 1985 with thirty persons grew to a membership of eight hundred by 1989. Here is their plan:

1. *Prayer*—We are establishing the life of each member by teaching each one how to pray and providing daily opportunities for corporate prayer.

2. *Care*—We are emphasizing care. Everyone needs someone to care for him [or her]. Using the vehicle of small care groups, we are nurturing a spirit of mutual love and care.

3. *Share*—We are encouraging each member to share the love of Christ with others. As we spread the good news of Jesus Christ we find fulfillment in our lives.

4. *Dare*—We challenge believers to have a daring faith in Christ. We believe God's creative power is sufficient for the situations of life we encounter daily.

5. *Prepare*—We are diligently and systematically preparing believers to fulfill their call as ministers. We believe that all Christians are to be equipped with the Word of God in their lives.[9]

Pastors, through classes, should communicate denominational history and beliefs for young people. Such information is helpfully transmitted to adult membership classes. Nothing, however, substitutes for clearly communicating that your congregation focuses on spiritual growth.

A fast-growing congregation in Kentucky developed a plan which involves church officers and the entire congregation in a unique, daily, prayer-connected group. Each minister is committed to praying for each elder *by name* every day. The elder is committed to praying for each of his or her flock families *by name* every day. Each deacon is committed to praying for each of his or her assigned families *by name* every day. Each flock family is encouraged to reverse the process—to pray for its deacon, elder, and ministers *by name* every day. What fantastic personal support possibilities this has! How much better this is than praying "Lord, bless this flock" once over lightly. No wonder the church grew. They let Christ in the door of their lives.

Action Possibility: Numerous types of prayer-chain and prayer-tree systems are available and useful. Many of these allow the pastor or another church leader to trigger the involvement of all members of the congregation in prayer for a specific person or need in a matter of minutes.

All of us are handicapped in one way or another. At some times more than at other times. Prayer is one of the many ways God can give us unexpected miracles to overcome these handicaps. That is equally true of entire congregations.

BEYOND THE FUND-RAISING MENTALITY

To celebrate laity Sunday, the leaders in a small church planned a worship service that would utilize the talents of several members. One of the teenagers was an excellent pianist, so they asked her to play for the offertory. Nobody thought to ask what music she had selected. As the offering plates circulated, she played Scott Joplin's rag time "The Entertainer," the theme from the movie *The Sting*.

The same kind of confusion happens when Christians discuss the word *stewardship*. Many people think stewardship means collecting money. This inaccurate definition leads many congregations to make a wrong turn at the clover leaf of church finances. Stewardship and fund-raising are different activities. Christian stewardship is a spiritual matter. Fund-raising is a mathematical, bill-paying matter. Stewardship is an attitude with which Christians approach life: It stems from their relationship with God. Fund-raising is getting money from people: It stems from the desire to underwrite the cost of operating a philanthropic organization.

In his Sermon on the Mount Jesus speaks of prayer, fasting, and giving as spiritual behaviors by which we relate to God. Many Christians, however, tend to see prayer and fasting as spiritual matters but view giving as an optional possibility for those who have some money left over after paying their bills. This unbiblical separation of giving from other spiritual growth behaviors is at least partly produced by our cultural experiences. Years of living in communities saturated with the fund-raising appeals of cookie-selling Girl Scouts, universities, and a thousand other worthy causes incline us to think of stewardship as fund-raising rather than what Jesus said it was—a spiritual matter.

The pastor-people ministry team in a vital congregation adopts attitudes and enacts methods that encourage members to develop sacrificial stewardship of financial, time, and talent resources. This involves much more than getting the money and the energy together to run the church. It involves helping people to grow in their spiritual relationship with God by the thoughtful, prayerful use of the principal resources that he has given them—money, time, and talent. A three-year-old girl said to her father on his way to the grocery store, "Daddy, bring me something that will last forever." The girl's request is a fine definition of stewardship. The giving of money, time, and talent brings a sense of meaning, purpose, and spiritual relatedness to God that lasts forever.

After walking through a cemetery, a man said, "Have you noticed how much meaning a dash can have? Born 1921—Died 1981. What a way to summarize a life—with a dash!" That will eventually describe the years of every person's life—a dash. We cannot stop our movement toward the final destination, but we can choose what we do with our dash. We can spend it on significant matters or on meaningless trivia. Thus a congregation's ministry of stewardship is a matter of ultimate importance—far more significant than fund-raising.

Shrouds have no pockets. We do not see Brinks trucks in funeral processions. Hearses do not pull U-Haul trailers. But stewardship lets us take it with us. "Lay up for yourselves treasures in heaven, where neither moth nor rust consumes and where thieves do not break in and steal" (Matt. 6:20). Through prudent stewardship, we can enter the abundant life of joy and meaning. Through stewardship, we can protect ourselves from being possessed by our possessions, thinking they are permanent and that they buy permanent security. Through stewardship, we can grow spiritually. Through stewardship, we create a meaningful dash.

The Bible makes 26 direct references to the words *steward* or *stewardship*. In the first verse where we encounter the word *stewardship*, Joseph, a Hebrew prisoner, is accountable to Pharaoh (Gen. 43–44). In the New Testament, stewardship often refers to the behavior of a slave who has been given responsibility over money, property, goods, or other slaves. Everywhere the word is used, it conveys the idea of a trustee, one to whom something of value is entrusted. Paul applies the concept of stewardship explicitly to himself as an apostle and implicitly to the church at large (I Cor. 4:1-2).

One of the most instructive stewardship texts is a story recorded by Mark. Jesus takes five loaves of bread and two fish and feeds 5,000 persons with them. Just before this incident, Jesus has sent the twelve out two by two to preach about the Kingdom and to heal the sick. When the apostles return to Jesus, he says, "Come away by yourselves to a lonely place, and rest a while" (Mark 6:31). But the group is seen leaving town. Soon, a huge crowd gathers at the place to which they have retreated for rest. Later that day, the disciples urge Jesus to send the 5,000 away to buy food. Jesus replies, "You give them something to eat" (Mark 6:37). Jesus takes what the disciples bring him—five loaves and two fish—and feeds 5,000 persons with it. We see exactly this kind of stewardship happening in a vital congregation. Because of their relationship with Christ, people bring what they have for use in God's kingdom. God miraculously multiplies our efforts for enormous usefulness.

How, exactly, can the pastor-people ministry team in today's church accomplish the task of encouraging members to develop sacrificial stewardship of financial, time, and talent resources? Their effectiveness in this ministry is determined by the degree to which they can answer yes to several questions.

1. Does our teaching about stewardship emphasize the need of the giver to give, rather than the need of the church to receive?

In Deuteronomy 16:16-17, we read "They shall not appear before the Lord empty-handed; [all] shall give as [they are] able, according to the blessing of the Lord your God which he has given you." The purpose of this injunction is not just to raise money to run the temple but is to strengthen the spiritual life of the donor. Too often, however, church leaders translate this spiritual matter into a dues-paying or a bill-paying matter. This is one of the reasons per capita financial giving in small congregations is almost always lower than it is in larger congregations. Smaller churches are much more likely to focus on paying the bills and to feel good about themselves when they succeed. They usually fail to realize that this attitude is actually holding their total giving down instead of lifting it up. The key spiritual question is never, What do the bills total? The key spiritual question is always, What does God call me to give as an expression of my relationship with God? Christians would need to give to others, even if churches as Christian communities had no overhead expenses whatever. Raising money to pay the bills is fund-raising. Stewardship is a much larger matter. When church leaders say, "Nobody likes to talk about money, but we have to pay the bills," they are transforming a crown jewel into cut glass costume jewelry.

2. Does our teaching about stewardship emphasize the need to give because of our gratitude to God, rather than because it is our duty as members?

A boy growing up in a tiny Midwestern town during the 1940s frequented the local movie theater. He thought he was spending big money by giving fourteen cents for a ticket and a chocolate ice cream fudgie. One evening, the owner came on stage at intermission with a special announcement. "If you people of this town do not start supporting this theater, it will close," he said in condemnatory tones. This proprietor was making two fundamental errors: (1) He was "preaching to the choir"—talking to the attenders rather than the nonattenders. (2) He was expecting his customers to base their behavior on feelings of duty rather than feelings of meaning.

Church leaders often make similar mistakes in their stewardship education methods. Research indicates that stewardship as "a duty of membership" scores seventh on the list of what motivates the average church member to give. When we focus on that and on "the church needs the money" (which is number six on the list of what motivates people to give), we hold the giving down instead of lifting it up. Number one on the list of what motivates people to give is "gratitude to God." When we emphasize that and number two on the list, "as a part of worship," people are much more likely to grow in their stewardship.[1]

3. Do we understand that people become good stewards because of preaching, teaching, and stewardship programs, rather than because they automatically start giving sacrificially of themselves when they start attending church?

An old cliche says, "Get the people there, and the money will come." This saying has a bit of truth in it, but not much. Yes, when more people attend worship, offerings increase. But people do not automatically become good stewards when they make the decision to become Christians or start attending worship. A little boy whose parents had not previously attended church watched everything with great interest. After three or four weeks passed, he tugged at his mother's sleeve one morning just after the offering plate went by. "I think I have this figured out," he said.

"What do you mean?" she asked.

"It must be one dollar for adults and fifty cents for children," he said.

He had noted one of those obvious truths that church leaders do not always see: Church attendance produces giving, but it does not automatically produce stewardship. Like many other Christian virtues, stewardship grows as a result of preaching, teaching, and programming designed to help encourage its growth.

Action Possibilities:

• Give persons in your congregations who tithe an opportunity to share their feelings about this with others. Instead of having "pitches" for various programs supported by the church budget, use the time (usually in worship services) for tithers to tell about their personal pilgrimage of giving, or about a memorable episode in giving, or how they made the early decisions that led them to a lifetime of giving. Advertising experts say that the most persuasive kind of advertisement is one satisfied customer telling a potential customer how happy he or she is with the product. The same principle applies in tithing education.

• Consider having someone from your stewardship committee visit the homes of all new members within three weeks after they join, leaving them a box of offering envelopes, a pledge card, and some kind of information that encourages percentage giving.

• Do a "wills emphasis" seminar every few years. At a church in Louisiana, not a single will was directed to the church in nine years . . . because nobody asked. After a wills emphasis seminar, estate giving-patterns changed. At the great Riverside Church in New York, Harry Emerson Fosdick printed at the bottom of every worship bulletin for decades—"Remember the church in your will." Several years after he began this practice, the church began receiving a bequest almost every week.

4. Do we understand that the failure of some people to grow spiritually stems from their failure to grow in stewardship?

Some church leaders assume that if they concentrate on programs that help people grow spiritually, gifts of money, time, and talent will automatically follow. This theory sounds so plausible! But some church members are blocked from spiritual growth until they decide to grow in their stewardship. And they may not grow in their stewardship until someone challenges them to do so. Jesus put it best:

"Where your treasure is, there will your heart be also" (Matt. 6:21).

5. Do we understand that people increase their level of financial giving because someone asks them to consider an increase?

What causes people to give is different from what causes them to increase their giving. Most *increases* in financial stewardship are based on the "stimulus-response" pattern that is so dependable in almost every aspect of human personality. People tend to continue in the same pattern of activity unless some new stimulus causes them to consider changing that pattern. Between 1980 and 1985, inflation increased church expenses in the United States by 26.7 percent—which is why many small churches began to experience financial difficulty during those years. Because such churches did not ask for increases in monetary stewardship, they did not receive them.

6. Do we understand that members are far more likely to reach sacrificial levels of giving if their congregation conducts an effective annual stewardship emphasis?

A pastor promised a member of her flock that she would be in the recovery room when he came out of the anesthesia following surgery. She was. As the man awakened through the foggy shroud of medication, he looked wildly about and said, "Where am I, and who are you?"

The minister took his hand and said, "Everything's all right. I'm your pastor."

"Oh, yes," said the patient, with a deep sigh, "just put me down for the same thing as last year." Without an effective annual stewardship emphasis, congregations get that kind of automatic response from large numbers of their members: "Put me down for the same thing as last year."

Napoleon had a regiment of soldiers he called his "Old Guard," because of their bravery and dependability. Once he stood before these soldiers and asked for a volunteer to undertake a hazardous mission. He warned them that the volunteer would risk losing his life. "I will turn my back," he said. "If anyone wishes to volunteer, he will step forward one pace." When Napoleon turned back around, not a single man had moved out of the ranks. But an officer reversed Napoleon's momentary disappointment with a quick salute and the report, "Sir, every man stepped forward one pace." Most Christians are capable of far higher levels of commitment than we expect. They will step forward in stewardship. But we have to ask them. An annual campaign is the most effective way to ask.

7. Do we understand that most church members do not like to visit the homes of other church members and ask them for money?

Small churches, and churches of every size in small towns, resist the use of annual stewardship programs. Most of them think that all stewardship campaigns involve calling in homes and asking for money. For them, this inevitably means calling on friends and relatives, and they do not want to endure that stress. Many of the most effective annual stewardship programs, therefore, do not ask members to call on other members and directly ask for money. Instead, people are asked to make their stewardship commitment to the operating budget as an act of worship during the Sunday morning service on "Consecration Sunday."

8. Do we recognize that even the best of stewardship programs must be changed every two or three years?

Research shows that virtually all types of stewardship programs decrease in effectiveness after a few years of use. The stimulus-response value declines as church members become more familiar with a particular program. Rather than feel challenged to grow spiritually, people become bored by the sameness and respond at the same levels. By this time, the church leaders will like the program, because they know how it works and find it easy to execute. In most cases, however, the percentage of increase in giving between each successive year keeps decreasing. Unless the leaders introduce a new type of program every few years, the stewardship tire gradually goes flat.

9. Do we keep financial stewardship programs separate from time-talent stewardship programs?

The whole pie of life involves stewardship, but it also has specific slices. Though there are rare exceptions, churches that conduct financial and time-talent stewardship campaigns in conjunction with each other can generally expect slimmer responses in both areas than if they conduct them separately. Putting these two kinds of stewardship together gives people the opportunity to say, "I can't give much money, but I will give time." Biblical stewardship involves both money *and* time-talent. Giving people the opportunity to exclude one or the other is therefore inappropriate. Regardless of the type of program we use, we need to ask the two questions separately: What does God expect of me regarding money? What does God expect of me regarding talent and time?

10. Do we understand that, in most churches with high per capita stewardship levels, the pastor plays a key leadership role in stewardship through preaching, teaching, and programming?

If the pilot decides to let the crew fly the plane alone—or if the crew takes a vote and decides it is not *spiritual* to let the pilot help with this particular part of the flight—the plane may or may not arrive at its destination. This does not mean that the pastor's "example" is of primary importance. He or she should give significantly and usually does, but this example is not enough. Nor is this even the critical factor in increasing a congregation's financial giving. In some congregations the minister is the biggest giver in the church, and nobody really cares. It doesn't influence anyone to higher levels of stewardship. The pastor must give leadership, but that does not mean that the pastor must give the largest gift or do all the work. Pastoral leadership means helping lay leaders to select and use the stewardship program that best fits their church and then helping them to implement their program effectively.

Even if churches did not need money to operate, they would still need the ministry of stewardship programs to help people keep their personal priorities straight. A United Methodist bishop once told about attending a country auction. It was a frosty December morning. The auction offered the usual conglomeration of belongings. There were four horses, twelve cows, and thirty sheep. Two wagon beds were piled high with tools, scrap metal, and rolled wire. Antique collectors nudged one another at the sight of a thirty-gallon copper kettle in which apple butter had been made the previous season. There was a brass bed adorned with a frayed canopy, and four bundles of used coat hangers. The table, piled high with glassware and bric-a-brac, included a two-by-three folding metal picture frame. One side was empty and the other held a blurry tintype.

The bishop said that the country auction points graphically to a basic truth about every one of us. One day soon, you and I will be called away. Relatives will hire an auctioneer (either literally or figuratively) and set up a hotdog stand in the tool shed. Nice people will buy soft drinks and coffee and bid on the apple butter kettle and Grandma's tintype.[2]

Viewed from the perspective of the country auction, stewardship is more easily recognized as a spiritual matter. What other goal in life is more significant than investing our lives in something that brings meaning, purpose, and a spiritual relatedness to God while we still can?

---------- X ----------

FROM SERVE-US TO SERVICE

The doctor was puzzled. "You should be recovering by this time," he said. "Have you followed my instructions?"

"Well, doctor," said the patient, "I've done most of them but I can't take that two-mile walk every morning that you recommended. I get too dizzy."

"What do you mean, 'dizzy'?" the doctor asked.

"Well, sir," said the patient, "I must have forgotten to tell you that I'm a lighthouse keeper."

Members of vital congregations keep the lamp lit for a dark world through preaching and teaching. But they do more than walk in circles in their lighthouse. They also climb down and row the lifeboats.

In the Great Commandment, Jesus instructs us to love God and our neighbors. In the parable of the good Samaritan, he defines the term *neighbor*. For Jesus, neighbor includes people who are outside our church, even people we do not know. Jesus binds our inward, spiritual journey toward God together with our outward, service journey toward other people. In his parable of the sheep and goats, he reviews a long list of hurting people—the sick, the naked, the prisoners, the hungry—and tells us that God will say to the unloving goat-types, "As you did it not to one of the least of these, you did it not to me" (Matt. 25:45).

A frustrated student slipped into the deserted university chapel and slumped into a pew. "All we have on this earth are problems and a bunch of dummies who will never figure out how to solve them," he said. "Even I could make a better world than this one."

Then, slicing through the stillness of the empty chapel, God said, "That is what you are supposed to do."[1]

Jesus scattered similar suggestions throughout his preaching and teaching. Activities based on this viewpoint are therefore found in every vital congregation. *The pastor-people team in a vital congregation adopts attitudes and enacts methods that reach out to help heal the hurts and meet the needs of people in the church, the community, and across the world.* The degree to which this happens in a congregation is determined by the degree to which its leaders can say yes to the following questions.

1. Do most of our members feel that genuine Christianity involves service to people outside the church?

In small congregations—and those of all sizes that have a long history of surviving against difficult odds such as community population changes, financial stress, or short-term pastors—members are tempted to adopt a "sanctuary mentality." People who think of their church in this way will view it as a place to which they withdraw for security and emotional protection. They do not see their church as a base camp for ministry to a hurting community. When several key leaders shift their thinking to unbiblical internal protection, a church begins to lose its vitality. Its service mentality deteriorates into a "serve-us" mentality. When churches are the "Body of Christ" with integrity, they serve their communities as well as their members. When they fail to care for their neighbors, they begin moving toward failure as a self-serving institution.

The Federal Aviation Administration has mandated warning systems for all airliners, which will prevent what happened to Flight 903 as it approached the Charlotte, North Carolina, airport. The pilot and co-pilot were engaged in general conversation about political and other matters when a signal began beeping and a red light started flashing. Someone flipped a switch to stop the noise, but it continued. The cockpit crew resumed their political discussion. The last words on the flight recorder were, "Where is the airport?" The crash was fatal. The plane had approached too low. The signals were warning the crew that they were too close to the ground. Churches need to similarly improve their selfishness warning systems. When they fly too close to their own self-interest, they crash.

2. Do we take the needs of people more seriously than the need to protect and preserve our building?

Most vital congregations house the ministry of at least one community group or activity within their building. A review of the history of congregations that do not serve their communities in this way often reveals a well-meaning property committee that has blocked this type of ministry. The committee members have seen themselves as protectors of the paint and the woodwork. Here is the best way to attack this sincere but misdirected attitude: Theologically speaking, selfishness is alien to the nature of the church and the mission Christ gave to it. Pragmatically speaking, churches that begin living only for themselves are starting a trip toward extinction. They will eventually die of spiritual asphyxiation because they lack the oxygen of love.

Action Possibility: To help your congregation face this question, ask the appropriate committee to discuss the church's attitude and policies regarding building use by outside groups. Although an open-door policy always brings some expense and frustration, it inevitably brings some ministry opportunities and some positive publicity. Grapple with the issue of whether your church is in business to protect itself from frustration or in business to serve the needs of people. This often moves a congregation toward more extroverted attitudes regarding building use.

3. Do we encourage our pastor to serve not just the church but the entire community?

Heavy involvement in civic and people-helping organizations in the community can easily get out of balance and cause a pastor to feel overextended. When carried to extremes, this busyness can lead to a neglect of essential leadership in other aspects of the congregation's ministry. But pastors can also be underextended in their community involvement. The smaller the community's population base, the more a church should encourage its pastor to serve the community. As well as genuinely helping people, this involvement increases congregational visibility. Although it should not be motivated for reasons of self-interest, community involvement helps give the church a caring, compassionate reputation, which tends to attract interest and new members.

4. Do we usually get involved in community crisis situations?

The note on the door said, "Sorry I missed you." Signed, "Opportunity." Some church doors are cluttered with such messages. But the leaders are so involved in a serve-us mentality that they do not notice.

Some of those opportunities involve helping families or individuals in crisis situations like fires, floods, or other personal tragedies. In responding to other opportunities, a caring pastor-people team must work with the city council or other governmental structures in order to correct action or inaction that adversely affects people.

A woman moved to a cave in the mountains to study with a respected spiritual guru. He gave her a stack of books to study and left her alone. Every morning he entered the cave carrying a wooden cane. Each morning, he asked her the same question: "Have you learned everything there is to know?"

Each morning, she said, "No, I haven't," and he struck her on the head with the cane.

This went on each day for months. Finally, one morning when he was about to hit her over the head again, she grabbed the cane in midair and wrested it away from him. The guru smiled. "Congratulations," he said. "You have graduated. You now know everything you need to know." "What do you mean?" she asked.

"You have learned that you will never learn all there is to know," he replied, "and you have learned how to stop the pain."[2]

Christians can never learn all there is to know about their faith. The smartest ones learn that. They keep working at their important ministry of learning and teaching, but they do not stop there. They also try to stop the pain. They know that the objective of Christian education is not just information but transformation, not just knowledge but action—loving action.

5. Do we seem to strike a good balance between our ministry to human physical need and our ministry to spiritual need?

In Matthew's Gospel, Jesus says, "Blessed are those who hunger and thirst for righteousness" (Matt. 5:6). Luke's Gospel puts forth the quotation more briefly and with a different emphasis: "Blessed are you that hunger" (Luke 6:21). Why does Matthew seem to be talking about spiritual hunger while Luke seems to be talking about physical hunger? We are not sure. Perhaps this is simply another example of Luke's tendency to "materialize the spiritual" into concrete caring acts directed toward the poor. Whatever the reason, the focus of Luke's Sermon on the Mount helps to remind us that people who authentically connect with Christ practice a love that involves both spiritual and physical dimensions.

Jesus did both things. He helped people both spiritually *and* physically-emotionally. He met the paralyzed man's greatest need: "My son, your sins are forgiven" (Mark 2:5). But he also met his physical need: "Rise, take up your pallet and go home" (Mark 2:11). Vital, growing churches also balance the energy they expend in these twin ministry tasks.

6. Does our church have a reputation for doing one particular community ministry extremely well?

No church can do everything that needs doing, but every church can do something that needs doing. Many growing congregations, especially those in smaller towns, have one specialty. They intentionally meet a particular human need in the community which is not being met by any other agency or church. Sometimes this is a mother's-day-out program. Sometimes it is a day care center. The list of possibilities is as varied as the needs of people and communities.

Action Possibilities:

• In our community, which of the following groups seem to have the greatest unmet social, personal, and spiritual needs: children, teenagers, young singles, young marrieds, adults, divorced persons, widowed persons, shut-ins, senior citizens, or some other group not covered in one of these categories?

• If these needs are not being met by other churches in the community, consider experimenting with them: an after-school or before-school care service or both (for working parents), a mother's day out, a preschool, or a parent-support group.

• Consider appointing a social concerns committee.

• If you wish to brainstorm about potential needs in the community, use the following method in an adult class, a fellowship dinner, or a board meeting.

1. After presenting a list of all the agencies you support and the special needs you meet within your building, give each person a set of 3 × 5–inch cards. Ask participants to write down one idea per card relating to things they would like to accomplish in the ministry of your church in the next five years. Allow ten minutes for this experience.
2. Next, ask participants to disclose their ideas to another person sitting nearby and listen to that person's ideas.
3. Then, instruct participants to star the card containing what they consider to be their own key idea.

4. Finally, ask everyone to stack his or her cards in order of importance, with the most important idea on top.
5. When all cards are returned, collate them and list them in sets of similar suggestions.
6. This process will surface potential new ministries. Is your congregation particularly well suited to giving leadership to one or more of these unmet community needs?

7. Do most of our leaders believe in extending our service to others beyond our town and county?

For ten years, Hubert and Marilyn Bankson have been hauling tons of clothing to needy people in Mexico. The wearables are donated by individuals, churches, charities, and retailers in Illinois and Iowa. Their local congregation, First United Methodist Church, Decatur, Illinois, donates $1,000 annually to help with expenses for the 2,000-mile round trip that the Banksons make five or six times each year. While in Mexico, the couple buys local crafts for sale back in Illinois, with the proceeds going to their church's mission fund. This is the philosophy on which they base their ministry: "We can't change all hunger and poverty, but you can take one little spot, and you can make a difference there."[3]

Research shows why the Banksons get such a positive response to their ministry. Church members think that the second most important thing a denomination needs to be doing for its congregations—after providing trained ministers—is the support of missions at home and abroad.[4] When we ask our members to support world mission causes, we are asking them to do something in which they already believe. If we do not ask them to do that, they will feel that something is missing in our church. They remember Jesus saying in the Great Commission that we should go into all the world, not just into all of Jerusalem and Samaria.

United States congregations have given many goods and much money to needy people overseas. And yet church leaders still have much to do. In some ways they are still miles behind congregations in other nations. Fourteen European nations and Canada rank ahead of the United States in the number of missionaries they support per capita. The United States is thus sixteenth with regard to missionary emphasis and holds approximately the same rank with regard to international aid programs.[5] In spite of the high percentage of United States citizens attending church each week, the spirit of isolation and inwardness is alive and well in the congregations.

The spectroscope is a device that breaks light rays into rainbow-like bands. These transverse lines of brightness and darkness vary owing to the heat and the chemical composition of the source of light and of any intervening vapor. By using a spectroscope, astronomers can sit in their observatories and learn the composition of and take the temperature of stars many light years away. In that same way, the molecular composition of a church is highly visible through its financial reports. Statisticians can look at the dollars a congregation gives to help those beyond its town and country and accurately describe the type of heart its members have. Mission giving figures tell whether Christians are selfish or generous, Christlike or greedy; whether they love others or themselves; whether they are interested in Christ's mission or their own.

8. Does our church cooperate with other churches in the community to help meet human needs that no one can meet alone?

Cooperation for the sake of saying that we are ecumenical can be little more than meaningless self-adulation. Cooperation for the sake of serving, on the other hand, is a genuine Christian activity.

When Thomas Jefferson was president, America had two hospitals—one in New York and one in Philadelphia. To be admitted, a patient had to be judged morally worthy. Unwed mothers and people with venereal diseases could not get in. Nor could someone with a "contagious" disease (a list that included tuberculosis and cancer).[6] This moral exclusion is one of the reasons that churches during the following centuries led in the building of hospitals. The hospitals were urgently needed acts of compassion.

Each new generation of church leaders faces a new challenge of human need. In each instance, a few in the congregation will say, "The church has no business being involved in that!" If the leaders wait until 100 percent of the members think this ministry should be done, then the congregation will do a total of nothing.

9. In our church, is the concept of service to the community and world often heard in Bible studies, sermons, and announcements?

What we teach, we tend to do. What we do not teach, we tend to neglect.

Action Possibility: Maintain a mission bulletin board in a conspicuous place in the church. Use maps of the world with pictures on them to highlight mission activities in the United States and other nations. Build a year's calendar of mission themes to be highlighted. These could be related to special offerings or to specific months. One might focus on international missions. Another might focus on retired ministers and missionaries. Another might focus on the church mission carried on nationally, and still another on the church's mission locally.

10. Are many of our members personally involved in serving our community and world in activities such as Meals on Wheels, Scouting, youth clubs, PTA, and politics?

Philosopher Walter Kaufmann said that the deepest difference between religious viewpoints is not the one between polytheism (belief in multiple gods) and monotheism (belief in one god). Nor is the difference between theism and atheism the greatest difference in viewpoints. The biggest chasm is between the people who do not feel other people's pain and those who do. Jesus said something similar. In his parable of the last judgment, the big test of religion was sensitivity to the needs of other people. This, rather than doctrinal belief, sent sheep in one direction and goats in the other.

Much Christian service is done, not through the church organization but through people who are motivated and empowered by their church participation. If this service is not happening, we may need to ask whether our church is providing genuine Christian motivation and empowerment. A little boy told his mother that he believed in Christ and wanted to be baptized. Since he was quite young, she was concerned. She wanted him to understand the significance of his decision. She explained that baptism brought some big responsibilities, like witnessing to his friends about his decision. "That won't work, Mom," he replied. "By the time I get to school, I'll be dried off, and they won't be able to tell." When members of a congregation are connected with Christ, people in the community can see it—even if they are dried off from baptism. It shows up in their serving.

Action Possibility: Encourage members to volunteer for local community agency work and recognize them in the worship service annually. Perhaps set a goal for a percentage of the church to be involved in this way.

11. Do we continually keep our members informed about our community and world-service ministries?

Some churches that have strong service ministries forget to tell their members about them. When we hide our good works from our people under a bushel of poor communication, we miss two great opportunities: (1) the chance to increase their self-esteem regarding their church; and (2) the chance to strengthen their desire to support those service ministries with time, talent, and money.

Action Possibility: Consider publicizing in a stronger way the various community agencies your congregation supports financially. Items scattered through the church paper or morning worship bulletin entitled "Did You Know?" can increase your members' awareness about this good work.

A woman in Georgia who works in a flower shop was sitting at her desk when a little boy came in. He looked to be seven or eight years old. "How much are the roses?" he asked. At the reply of $50, his eyes got big. "How much is six?" he asked.

After the answer, he wanted to know the price of one. The woman said, "$6.75 in a vase."

"I have been savin' money for my mama's birthday for a long time," he said.

"How much money do you have?" the clerk asked. "We have carnations, they are much cheaper than roses."

He pulled a handful of coins out of his pocket. "I've been savin' a long time," he said.

She saw that he had less than two dollars, not enough for anything they sold. "I have just the thing," she said enthusiastically. Going to the back of the shop, she soon returned with several carnations in a piece of paper—along with some baby's breath and what florists call "leather leaf," a kind of fern that makes flowers look pretty.

As he was leaving the shop, face aglow, she remembered that she had forgotten to give him a card. She wrote on it, "Happy Birthday, Mom," and signed his name. Dashing out the door, she caught up with him. "The look in his eyes at that moment," she said, "was worth more than the money we made all day."

The Bible has a name for this transaction, *grace*—an undeserved, unmerited, unearned gift. Because the people in vital congregations have received this gift, they can offer it to others.

RESOURCES

Most of the resources recommended in *The Vital Congregation* can be obtained from local bookstores or from denominational publishing houses.

You may also want to call or write the appropriate departments in the national or regional offices of your denomination for a listing of the resources they produce in each of these areas of ministry.

1. Your Most Important Employee

Ask the church board or some other key leadership group to engage in a three-session study-discussion of the little booklet by Speed B. Leas, *A Layperson's Guide to Conflict Management* (Washington, D.C.: The Alban Institute). It provides a simple, clear analysis of causes and prescriptions for handling conflict situations in congregations. In some churches, inviting an outside leader to lead these discussions has proved helpful—since that person has no emotional involvement in present or past conflict patterns.

For help in developing a congregational mission statement, see *Revitalizing the 20th Century Church* by Lloyd M. Perry and Norman Shawchuck (Chicago, Ill.: Moody Press).

For insights regarding how to move beyond the patterns often found in congregations where the senior minister has served more than ten years, see *New Visions for the Long Pastorate* by Oswald, Hinand, Hobgood, and Lloyd (Washington, D.C.: The Alban Institute).

The video discussion entitled *Developing a Vital Congregation*, and its accompanying *Participant's Guide*, by Herb Miller (Lubbock, Tex.:

Net Press), provide six, two-hour planning sessions with a church cabinet, administrative council, or other leadership group.

2. The God Connection

Pastors, worship committees, and evangelism committees will find significant insights in a booklet by Gary Miller, pastor of a fast-growing United Church of Christ congregation in Algonquin, Illinois: *The Worship Experience in a Growing Church* (St. Louis: Church Leadership Resources).

Sunday Morning Alive by Shirley Pollock (Lima, Ohio: C.S.S. Publishing Co., Inc.). This stimulating seventy-six-page resource provides delightful insights, illustrations, and practical ideas that can be used in the areas of (1) the sermon, (2) forms of worship, (3) welcomes, (4) lay ministries, (5) recognition, and (6) special services.

Hospitality in a Growing Church Training Guide for Welcomers, Ushers, and Teachers by James W. Biddle and R. Alan Johnson (St. Louis: Church Leadership Resources).

Net Results is a monthly journal of new ideas in evangelism and church vitality. Write to *Net Results*, 5001 Avenue N, Lubbock, TX 79412-2917; or call 1-800-638-3463.

Obtain and use copies of the *Net Results* article "Suggested Questionnaire for Those Who Have Visited Our Church" in order to gain more insights regarding how to strengthen the value of your worship service.

Obtain and use the *Net Results* article "Twenty Questions for Your Church Bulletin" as a way of improving the value of your worship service for visitors.

3. Climate Controls the Crops

Two resources in wide use for study by Care Corps members are (1) The leader's guide and participant's handbook in *A Ministry of Caring* by Duane A. Ewers (Nashville, Tenn.: Discipleship Resources and (2) *Tools for Active Christians* by Herb Miller (St. Louis, Mo.: CBP Press).

The Stephen Ministries, 1325 Boland, St. Louis, MO 63117, has an excellent training program for setting up care systems.

Lead Consultants, Inc., under the direction of John Savage, conducts many types of helpful workshops and training events throughout the United States on the subject of ministry to inactive members. To obtain information about this, write to P.O. Box 664, Reynoldsburg, OH 43068, or phone 1-614-864-0156.

Coming Home for Christmas by Herb Miller (Lubbock, Tex.: Net Press), equips leaders for both remedial and preventive work with inactive members. In addition to providing a six-week, step-by-step program for reactivating inactive members, it contains a two-hour training session that shows leaders how to make visits to the homes of persons who are just starting on the flight path toward inactivity. When used in its entirety—either at Christmas time or Easter time—it will recover 15 percent of inactive members, including some who may have been inactive for ten years or more. When the two-hour training module is used, and when leaders organize to make that type of visit to the home within six weeks of the time people drop out of worship, 85 percent will return and continue as active members.

To increase the general understanding of church leaders about the reasons people become inactive in churches and what can be done to prevent that, obtain a copy of the video entitled *Dealing with Inactive Members* by Herb Miller (Lubbock, Tex.: Net Press) and have it viewed by several of the leadership groups in your church. As understanding grows regarding the causes and remedies for inactivity, leaders will begin to support the idea of developing effective procedures to deal with it.

4. The Beehive Principle

To involve the maximum number of new members in ministry, look at two resources: (1) *Every Member in Ministry* by John Ed Mathison (Nashville, Tenn.: Discipleship Resources); and (2) the new-member assimilation section in *Fishing on the Asphalt* by Herb Miller (St. Louis, Mo.: CBP Press).

The video and booklet *Identifying Your Spiritual Giftabilities* by Herb Miller (Lubbock, Tex.: Net Press) can be used for a forty-minute presentation and discussion for two sessions in adult Sunday school classes or other groups—or as a two-hour workshop for adult groups of any size (which any pastor or layperson can lead). This benefits individuals in the church by helping them discover the gifts God has given them for ministry. It benefits churches by motivating more individuals to use their giftabilities to get more of God's work done in more effective ways.

Small congregations frustrated with trying to use a committee system, which fits better in large churches where there are numerous persons available to fill the committees, may wish to experiment for one year with the system recommended in the section on administration in *Tools for Active Christians* by Herb Miller

(St. Louis, Mo.: CBP Press). This approach significantly reduces conflict while increasing democratic participation in decision making, requires fewer members to operate, and involves more members in ministry.

The larger the congregation, the more likely it is to benefit from the type of training in programs to equip laypersons with ministry and leadership skills provided by the Stephen Ministries, 1325 Boland, St. Louis, MO 63117; 1-314-645-5511.

Obtain and study "How to Prevent Lay Leader Burnout," by Roy Oswald and Jackie McMakin (Washington, D.C.: The Alban Institute). It lists the six primary causes of burnout and the nine warning signs.

5. Loading the Plane

Consider using one of the following books in adult Sunday school classes as a means of raising consciousness and increasing evangelism motivation: *Faith-Sharing* by H. Eddie Fox and George E. Morris (Nashville, Tenn.: Discipleship Resources); *The Contagious Congregation* by George G. Hunter III (Nashville, Tenn.: Abingdon Press); *The Master's Plan* by Win Arn (Moravia, Calif.: Church Growth, Inc.); *Evangelism's Open Secrets* by Herb Miller (St. Louis, Mo.: CBP Press).

Church Advertising: A Practical Guide by Steve Dunkin (Nashville: Abingdon Press), is one of the best practical overviews of this subject.

Life Stream Evangelism, 7275 South Broadway, Littleton, CO 80122, provides a church brochure design service for congregations.

Make a three-year plan in which two times each year you use one of the five methods for helping church members increase the number of invitations they extend. These five methods are found in *Additional Resources Packet, Blueprints for Evangelism and Church Growth* (Lubbock, Tex.: Net Press). Do not use any combination of the five methods more than two times each year. They become ineffective if overused.

6. Taking Down the Fences

Obtain a copy of the best-selling book by Lyle Schaller, *Assimilating New Members* (Nashville: Abingdon Press).

One of the best methods for new member assimilation is found in the book *Every Member in Ministry* by John Ed Mathison (Nashville,

Tenn., Discipleship Resources). Mathison, pastor of one of the fastest growing United Methodist congregations in America, offers not just new insights, but a completely new model for immediately involving new members in a group and a role.

7. Putting the Wheels On

The video entitled *Growth Principles and Methods for Adult Sunday School Classes* by Herb Miller (Lubbock, Tex.: Net Press) is most valuable when a church asks each adult class to spend one session viewing and discussing the twelve principles and numerous methods outlined in it.

View and use the principles and methods in the video entitled *Youth Sponsor Workshop* by Herb Miller (Lubbock, Tex.: Net Press).

Plan at least one completely new program, group, or event during the Lenten season or autumn of the next twelve months. Among the countless possibilities available for Bible study and discussion groups are *Building a Meaningful Life with the Carpenter's Twenty Megatruths* by Herb Miller (Lubbock, Tex.: Net Press); *Actions Speak Louder Than Verbs* by Herb Miller (Nashville: Abingdon Press); *How Not to Reinvent the Wheelbarrow* by Herb Miller (Nashville: Abingdon Press), and *Discovery II* by Herb Miller (Lubbock, Tex.: Net Press).

8. The Best Kind of Networking

Information on the excellent program *The Walk to Emmaus* is available from the Upper Room, P.O. Box 189, Nashville, TN 37202-1089; 1-615-340-7227.

Obtain and review the *Singles Ministry Handbook*, Douglas L. Fagerstrom, Ed. (Wheaton, Ill.: Victor Books).

Obtain and review *How to Start a Singles Ministry* by Britton Wood (Nashville, Tenn.: Broadman Press). This audiocassette covers the basics of how to get a singles group off the runway, and more important, how to keep it flying with color. Since many singles groups founder at the beginning stages (or cannot figure out how to taxi out of the hangar), the cassette is invaluable for the pastor who has one or several persons say, "We need to start a singles group. How do we do that?"

The billfold-size folder entitled *The Secret to Abundant Living: Learning How to Ask* by Herb Miller (Lubbock, Tex.: Net Press) has assisted leaders in many congregations in helping thousands of people establish a daily prayer life in which they experience God's peace, joy, and power.

9. Beyond the Fund-raising Mentality

The most effective annual stewardship campaigns receive the "Estimate of Giving" cards *before* the budget is designed. The *Consecration Sunday Stewardship Program* by Herb Miller (Lubbock, Tex.: Net Press) usually achieves first-year increases in giving of between 20 and 30 percent. It focuses on having people complete commitment cards as an act of worship during a Sunday morning service.

10. From Serve-Us to Service

For ideas and possible consultation on community service ministries, write to the Reverend Steve Edwards, Community and Senior Services, 1301 W. Louisiana, Midland, TX 79701. That organization is one of the finest examples in America of churches of various denominations linking together with the business interests of the community to provide a ministry to senior citizens and needy persons of various kinds.

139

NOTES

1. Your Most Important Employee

1. Bernie S. Siegel, "How to Heal Yourself," in an interview by Michell Lodge, *Ladies' Home Journal* (June 1989), p. 108.

2. Thomas R. Horton, *What Works for CEOs: Interviews with 16 Chief Executives* (New York: Random House, 1986), interview with Richard A. Zimmerman.

3. Martin Marty, *Context* (December 1, 1988), p. 2.

4. Gerald Kennedy, *Have This Mind* (New York: Harper and Bro., 1948), p. 183.

2. The God Connection

1. *Anglican Digest*, Diocese of Toronto, quoting Archbishop William Temple in 1944.

2. Thomas D. Morgan, *Congregational Tools for Effective Evangelism: An Overview* (The Divisions for Life and Mission in the Congregation and Service and Mission in America, The American Lutheran Church, 422 South Fifth Street, Minneapolis, MN 55415).

3. Cynthia W. Sayre and Herb Miller, *The Christian Church (Disciples of Christ) New Member Study,* a study initiated by Harold Johnson, executive for the department of evangelism and membership of the Division of Homeland Ministries of the Christian Church (Disciples of Christ), Indianapolis, November 1985.

4. Carl F. Reuss, *Survey of Lutherans* (Minneapolis: American Lutheran Church, 1985).

5. T. Garrott Benjamin, Jr., "How Second Christian Church Has Grown," *Net Results* (November 1981), pp. 1-2.

6. Herb Miller, *How to Build a Magnetic Church* (Nashville: Abingdon Press, 1987), p. 48.

7. William B. Franklin, "Two Sides of Silver," *The Christian Ministry* (May 1983), p. 35.

8. Donald Macleod, *The Problem of Preaching* (Philadelphia: Fortress Press, 1987).

9. Frederick A. Norwood, ed., *Doctrines and Discipline of The Methodist Episcopal Church in America*, facsimile edition (Rutland, Vt.: Academy Books, 1979), pp. 120-21. Quoted in *Rekindling the Flame*, William Willimon and Robert Wilson (Nashville: Abingdon Press, 1987), p. 120.

3. Climate Controls the Crops

1. Jonathan Swift, *Thoughts on Various Subjects*, 1706.

2. Frank Grazian, *Communication Briefings*, April 1989, p. 5.

4. The Beehive Principle

1. Thom Albin, "Four Types of Church Groups," *Net Results*, (September 1986).

2. Richard B. Wilke, *Signs and Wonders* (Nashville: Abingdon Press, 1989), p. 88.

3. Ibid.

4. Roy Oswald and Jackie McMakin, *How to Prevent Lay Leader Burnout* (Washington, D.C.: The Alban Institute, 1984).

5. Loading the Plane

1. Ron Elbourne, "Parson's Pitch," Glen Waverly, Australia, newspaper column sometime in late 1988 or early 1989.

2. John Wesley, *Letter to Samuel Walker*, 1754.

3. Herbert Vander Lugt, *Our Daily Bread*, June–August 1989, Radio Bible Class, Grand Rapids, MI 49555.

4. *U.S. News and World Report*, September 28, 1987, p. 13.

5. Douglas W. Johnson and George W. Cornell, *Punctured Preconceptions* (New York: Friendship Press, 1972). A summary of the opinions of 24,184,335 Protestants (one-hour interviews with 3,454 of them).

6. George Gallup, Jr., *The Unchurched American—10 Years Later* (Princeton, N.J.: Princeton Religion Research Center, 1988), p. 53,

and *The Unchurched American* (Princeton, N.J.: Princeton Religion Research Center, 1978), p. 18.

7. Avery T. Willis, Jr., Part 1 of "Strategy for Discipling in the Local Church." Presented at the American Festival of Evangelism, July 29, 1981.

8. *Enablement Newsletter*, James L. Lowery, Jr., ed., February 1988, quoting Bishop Richard Grein, who was then Episcopal Bishop of Kansas and is now Episcopal Bishop of New York. *Enablement Newsletter* is a division of Enablement, Inc., 14 Beacon Street, Room 707, Boston MA 02108; 617-742-1460.

6. Taking Down the Fences

1. *American Demographics* (August 1989).

2. Joseph Campbell, *The Power of Myth*, with Bill Moyers (New York: Doubleday, 1988), p. 22.

3. Flavil R. Yeakley, *Why Churches Grow* (Monrovia, Calif.: Christian Communications, 1979), p. 54.

7. Putting the Wheels On

1. In *Better Homes and Gardens* (January 1988).

2. A study reported in *Emerging Trends* published by the Princeton Religion Research Center in 1986, in which there are in-person interviews with 1,522 adults, eighteen and older, which were conducted in 1984.

3. *Pulpit Helps* (June 1989), quoting from the *Chattanooga News-Free Press*.

4. Trends revealed by comparing two studies of religious beliefs and behavior among U.S. adults—one conducted in 1978 and the other in 1988. Both surveys, *The Unchurched American, 1988* and *The Unchurched American, 1978*, were conducted by the Gallup organization.

5. Bernie Siegel, *Ladies' Home Journal* (June 1989), p. 178. See also Siegel's best-selling book, *Love, Medicine, and Miracles* (New York: Harper & Row, 1986).

6. James Finley, "Sharing a Vision, Creating an Agenda," (Retreats International, Inc., Box 1067, Notre Dame, IN 46556), p. 2.

7. George Roche, "The Litigious Society: Culture Crisis," *Executive Speeches*, July 1988 (Joe Taylor Ford, ed., *The Executive Speechwriter Newsletter*, Emerson Falls, St. Johnsbury, Vermont 05819).

8. Kent B. Hill, "Lack of Spiritual Food Identified as Major Factor in Church Declines," *National Christian Reporter* (March 31, 1989).
9. Bernie Siegel, *Ladies' Home Journal* (June 1989), p. 138.
10. George Gallup, Jr., as reported in the *Lubbock Avalanche-Journal* (May 1987).

8. The Best Kind of Networking

1. John Wesley, *Through the Year with Wesley*, comp. and ed. Frederick C. Gill (Nashville: Upper Room, 1983), p. 23.
2. In *Better Homes and Gardens* (January 1988).
3. *American Demographics* (November 1987), p. 59.
4. *John Naisbelt's Trend Letter* (April 13, 1989).
5. *Pulpit Humor* (July 1989).
6. *Pulpit Helps* (July 1989).
7. *National and International Religion Report* (April 25, 1988), p. 8.
8. Ronald Schiller, "How Religious Are We?" *Reader's Digest* (May 1986), p. 102.
9. Advertisement in *Lubbock Avalanche-Journal* (March 25, 1989).

9. Beyond the Fund-raising Mentality

1. *Punctured Preconceptions* by Douglas W. Johnson and George W. Cornell (New York: Friendship Press, 1972), p. 128. A summary of the opinions of 24,184,335 Protestants (one-hour interviews with 3,454 of them).
2. Webb B. Garrison, *Creative Imagination in Preaching* (Nashville: Abingdon Press, 1960), pp. 74-75.

10. From Serve-Us to Service

1. Martin E. Marty, *Context* (August 15, 1989), quoting from *Sunday Sermons*, a United Methodist clergy magazine.
2. Melody Beattie, *Codependent No More* (New York: Harper & Row, 1987), p. 7.
3. *The United Methodist Reporter* (January 13, 1989).
4. Johnson and Cornell, *Punctured Preconceptions*, p. 101.
5. Robert T. Coote, *Mission Handbook*, 13th Ed. (Monrovia: Missions Advanced Research Communication's Center, a division of World Vision International, 1986).
6. *The Executive Speechwriter Newsletter*, vol. 4, no. 1, p. 11 (Emerson Falls, St. Johnsbury, Vermont 05819).